SOCIAL MEDIA

MARKETING

COMPLETE GUIDE

2023

2 Manuscripts: Social Media Marketing

2023 + Social Marketing for beginners

2023

TOM RUELL

Copyright © Tom Ruell 2023,

All rights reserved

Table of Contents

Introduction 4

Chapter 1: LinkedIn Strategy 52

Chapter 2: Instagram Marketing 76

Chapter 3: The Tik-tok Prospect 99

Chapter 4: The Pinterest Prospect 114

Chapter 5: Facebook Marketing 128

Conclusion 144

Introduction 149

Chapter 1: Startup 155

Chapter 2: Instagram Marketing Strategy 201

Chapter 3: Tiktok 221

Chapter 4: The Ultimate Marketing Strategy 231

Chapter 5: The LinkedIn Market 250

Chapter 6: Pinterest as media platform 279

Conclusion 301

Introduction

Since 2020, companies have basically been forced to take digital marketing seriously with the pandemic. Many companies couldn't rely on foot traffic anymore to generate revenue because of the lockdowns and social distancing. This led to a colossal explosion and demand for digital marketing, and social media is one of the best channels for businesses to leverage. Sprout's Social's 2021 index found that nine out of 10 consumers will buy from brands they follow on social media. 86% will choose that brand over a competitor, and 85% will buy from that brand more often. This means competition is expected to grow, so will consumers' willingness to use this marketing channel to make buying decisions. You can expect social media to get even more competitive over the coming year. As companies start getting better and more competitive in social media marketing, you'll have to compete for attention far more than before. So, here are some things that you can do to compete on a level playing field. Now, a few key factors will differentiate you from your competition. The first one is;

==respond to customer service questions promptly.==

Don't you just hate it when you hit someone up and have issues, and it takes them a few days to get back. You want an answer right then? No one wants to wait, even an hour. Time is everything. Many social media users are engaging with their brands beyond just following up. You need to _demonstrate responsiveness and answer the customers in a timely fashion._

Demonstrate an understanding of what they want and need? You should keep customers in mind as you create content because it's all about servicing them and providing stuff for them. It's like I meet some people who are like, oh, I got the best business idea. I'm going to make some cupcakes. Most of the time, I'm like, this is cool, but is there a demand for it? It may taste good, but if there's really not a demand for it, it won't do well. It's not about you and your brand. It's about how you can serve your customers and your audience. Knowing what your potential customers want and need is going to differentiate you from all these brands and other brands that are just churning out content for the sake of highlighting their products, their services, and their own brands. An excellent way to measure this is by looking at different content pieces and seeing which one gets the most engagement. As you discover the types of content that tend to perform well, just do more of them. But here's the thing that no one really talks about in marketing. For those who don't do well, don't do them again. Test them out again once in a while because trends change, and people may like them again. And then, if you do that, you'll keep staying ahead of the curve, and you'll start doing better.

Create more culturally relevant content. Today, we can see more and more brands creating content around cultural events that mobilize people's attention, like Black Lives Matter and the Me-Too movement and even some mainstream sports events like the Olympics. So when you create content around some of these moments and events, especially those you want to support and believe in, no one is doing anything unethical. It's great to keep events, different people, cultures, and genders. And what you want to do is leverage them and show that you're there. And then do not just leverage them to make a financial profit, but also help people. That will resonate with them and create a win-win situation, but you should only do it if you genuinely care. Don't just do something for marketing. Do something because you genuinely care. You should be listening to what's drawing your audience's attention and create content that resonates with those topics. That includes putting out user-generated content because user-generated content is impressive. Also, create educational content about products or services that you're offering.

This is the difference between selling and showing up. Selling is great, but you want to show up and generate sales for yourself. When it comes to your product, It should be about educating and putting things first for others. For example, if you have some fantastic makeup product and your product helps people not just put on the makeup quicker, but just take it off really quick. If you can show how your own product can get off really quickly in one circular wipe, you're going to get sales. You should be able to offer your product in a way that revolves around your customer's problems, needs, and wants, and not just try to sell to them but help them solve those problems. As a product provider, you should actively engage with your clients by responding to their comments questions and even looking at their profiles. This will help you do better.

The Digital Market Sphere

This book will discuss advanced Social Media Marketing and manage your digital content and social media. Gaining tips on how to use online platforms to canalize traffic and grow your business and all of this will be done looking through the lens of social media marketing.

Let us first look at the best digital marketing tools out there, the ones that have gained a solid track record over time, the ones that are popular, and the ones that we foresee as being the go-to tools for the future. So, past, present, and future digital marketing tools are how to look at it.

SEO (Search Engine Optimization)

Search engine optimization or organic search has a mixture of paid and free. Different platforms offer SEO services. Now, let's look into some of these platforms. There's SEMrush. There's also a google free search console. If you don't have an SEO platform, you should look into the google search console. There's also google keyword planner, which is actually situated under google ads and so if you're running google campaigns on google search network or even the display network, you have access to a great tool called keyword planner, and if you know anything about SEO, you'll know that using Google's keyword planner is a good tool. Moz is a freemium tool, meaning they have a free trial that you can sign up for to test drive it, but it's another SEO platform, and it does cost money. These are all surface explanations. Now, let's go forward and dive deeper into SEOs and also try to understand why we use some of these tools.

The first reason would be to find relevant keywords; not only do we want to find relevant keywords, but we also want to find relevant keywords with high volume and low competition, we wouldn't want to find non-relevant keywords with increased competition and low volume, that wouldn't make sense. So, we need a tool to help us put it all together, and the means of choice for this material is Google's keyword planner. It helps us hone in on keywords we may be interested in optimizing, and this is because it is relevant and has a high volume and low competition.

Google Keyword planner

The idea of using Google's keyword planner is one we want to get an idea of what other keywords are out there that are relevant, so it helps stimulate some ideas for relevancy

we can get an average monthly search volume, so we want to know on average over the past 12 months how many search queries you can expect from this keyword and then

You can get a sense of the competition; how competitive is this keyword? So if I try to optimize for this keyword and want to rank for it organically, is it competitive? If it's competitive, it's probably going to take me a bit longer to be found for this keyword on page one of google.

So, that's the whole idea behind Google's keyword planner and note that you could change some of the settings here so if you want to choose a different language, okay you can hone in on a longer or shorter period you can even select a specific location

Moz (PAID)

Moz has an embedded tool called "keyword explorer." Moz provides us with the volume of users honing a particular keyword, giving us the competition. It also gives us other keywords that we can potentially hone in on.

Moz delivers many other analyses related to the keyword and provides some keyword suggestions. You have to keep in mind that when you optimize, you're optimizing a page for more than one keyword, so you want to be able to have an excellent portfolio of diverse relevant keywords with high search volume and low difficulty, and then you want to be able to identify those keywords that your competitors are ranking.

Google search console

This tool is free and a must; if you're going to work on SEO, you need to be working in the google search console, so the whole key behind the google search console is your website, and you need to get that site verified.

The social media sphere

You know you need to be on social media to implement any social media marketing strategy. YouTube, Facebook, Twitter, Instagram. Some of the most popular sites out there on the web. Even Snapchat. Even though Instagram is crushing it, it's still doing really well. They have over a hundred million active users daily. But as a beginner, all of this is overwhelming and complicated. So how do you start? We will discuss how to get started with social media as a beginner.

The first thing you need to do is <u>pick the right social network</u>. Yes, there's a lot of them. Whether it's Facebook, LinkedIn, or Twitter, it's up to you on which network you want to be on. You could be on all of them, but if you're in all of them, you're not going to spend enough time to make these profiles unique. You don't want half-cooked content on half-baked platforms. In other words, you don't want to be on LinkedIn and do a mediocre job. You don't wanna be on Facebook and do a mediocre job. It's better not to be on them than to do a mediocre job. Because doing a mediocre job will get you no reach, I kid you not. Social media five-six years ago was way easier to leverage to get traffic from. Nowadays, their algorithms are so strict because there's so much competition they're looking for the cream of the crop.

In other words, if you're not the best of the best, you're not going to do well. So you need to pick the right social network. And what's right for me may not be suitable for you. The way you pick the social network is to look up what space you're in. If you're in B2B, the chances are LinkedIn is going to be the best social network for you. Twitter is also another promising social network for B2B, but LinkedIn typically is better. If you're in B2C, Facebook does really well, Instagram does really well, YouTube does really well. Funny enough, YouTube works for both B2B and B2C.

Now here's the thing, you also have to look at what content type you like creating. Are you really good with videos? If so, you probably want to start with YouTube or LinkedIn. [→ TOUR/TRAILERY INTERVIEWS] Facebook is much more competitive. YouTube, you can get longevity; even if you don't have an audience or have a subscriber pool, you can get more traffic over time. Because Facebook people don't really search on there. YouTube people perform searches all day long for videos, and these contents can continually get views if you rank higher. If you're going after the older demographic, Facebook is fantastic. If you're [TIKTOK?] going after the younger demographic, Instagram and Snapchat are amazing. So now that you have a rough idea of which social network to go after.

Now that you have the right one, the second thing you need to do is start creating content. Yes, you're like, hey, I have no friends and no following. It doesn't matter; no one will follow if you don't have any content. So start creating content. That starts off with completing your profile, [REVIEW] Facebook, Twitter, Instagram all of them have profiles. You need to complete everything from a username to your email address to a really proper nice image to a description of who you are or your company. If you don't complete your profile, you're not giving people a reason to follow. And when you're completing your profile, talk about the benefits that people will experience from following you or subscribing to your page. But as I mentioned, it's all about creating content. So it starts with the profile, and then it gets to content.

If you're unsure what content to create, you need to check out your competition. We all have competitors. Even if you're in a new space, let's say you're Uber and revolutionizing the taxi industry where your competition would be the taxi industry. So you look at what your competition is doing on social media. Now I know Uber is already around; they're a multi-billion dollar company. But give me an example of if I was creating uber from day one, that would be my competition. You look at your closest competitors. It could be in direct competition but still your closest competitors. You want to see what content is doing well for them and what contents are not. That'll give you an idea of what you should do more of and what you shouldn't is much of. If you don't know how to create content, it could be as simple as status updates, you pulling out your phone recording a video of yourself. Sharing some links. And if you're not sure what links to share, you can go to *buzzsumo.com*. Type in any keywords from your industry; it'll show you all the popular articles. That shows you what people like on Facebook, Twitter, and social sites, which will give you an idea of what kind of content will resonate with that social network and what doesn't.

Now that you're creating content, the next thing you need to do is build a connection, and you need to build a connection with people; it's a social network. Just because you're on a computer doesn't mean you're not connecting with humans. So make sure you're friending all the people you know, following them. You're engaging, right? You're building connections. So if it's your friend already, like there's someone you know in person, you can just invite them to friend you on Facebook or follow you on Twitter. If it's someone you don't know, you're going to have to work more to build that connection. And here's how you do this. You look for all the people in your space who post status updates. If they have questions respond to them, help them out. If they have articles feel free and share them if you think they're valuable, right? You can repost, re-share, whatever it may be. If other people on these channels' fan pages are related to your industry, even if it's your competitors and they're asking questions, you can respond to them and help them out. That's how you build a connection. Even when you're posting on your own page, when someone responds with a question or a comment, you should acknowledge that they're there. Thank them for leaving a comment.

Respond when they have a question. That's how you engage. And what I found is over time, as you engage, what you'll see is a lot of people will come back over to your site, they'll follow you. You'll engage deeply with them, and they'll become a loyal diehard follower. It's not just about growing your number and having 1,000 followers or 10,000 followers. Which then gets me into my last tip. And the last tip is don't go for follower count. It's all about having valuable connections, personal ones. Because if your first 100 fans or followers aren't that engaged with you, all these social networks have it in their algorithms where they're looking at a percentage. So if you have a million fans, but only 1,000 engage, they're like, " Whoa, this is a terrible engagement rate. We shouldn't show your content to anyone 'cause no one likes it. But if you had a hundred followers and every single one liked it, shared it, and commented, they did all three of those things; social networks like Facebook are going to be like this, this content is impressive; it needs to go viral because everyone loves it. So it's not about having the most amount of fans; it's about having the most amount of engaged fans. If someone's not going to engage, you don't want them. Don't just pay models to talk about you to get more followers. It's about having the most relevant diehard fans.

Don't push people to your business from day one. Within three months or six months, by all means, you can start talking about your business, slowly mentioning it. Try to get people over to your site and us customers. You can do simple things like just sharing a link. But you don't wanna do that from day one. Why would you wanna promote your business when no one's following you? They're not engaged. If you walked up to a random stranger on the street and you said, "Hey, my name is John. "I know that you buy toilet paper "because everyone uses toilet paper. "Would you like to buy my toilet paper?" They're going to be like, "You're crazy, who are you? "We don't want to buy anything for you." You need to build a connection. No one's going to buy from you until you build that relationship. So don't promote your business until three to six months. I'm to the extreme where I like waiting nine months to a year. But again, you can do it within three to six months. You can promote your business instantly if you're doing advertising from day one. But if you're trying to build up everything organically. You can't promote your business from day one.

These are the most common platforms, although there are hundreds of others. When we talk about social media marketing and competition, we will notice that there are many different types of social media platforms, ranging from microblogging to video-sharing platforms like YouTube, networking platforms like LinkedIn, bookmarking sites, and content sharing sites like Reddit and Q&A sites like Quora. Let us now turn our attention to one of the most prominent social media networks, Facebook.

Facebook is evenly matched or say distributed between males and females, so if I'm skewing my target towards the older or younger ones as my target audience, and half as female and half as male, then I know somewhere in there, whomever I'm targeting is going to be on Facebook just based on these numbers here, so your demographic is likely to be on Facebook. Now that Facebook permits video content to upload films all day, you may publish your YouTube videos on Facebook; like most platforms, videos tend to give more interaction in capitalized sectors.

Facebook has an average of (2.27 billion) two-point two seven billion monthly active users. That number is fluctuating since we talk about billions of monthly active users. Up to 88% of all users are on mobile, so what does that tell you? That means you that Facebook has an app and that app is viral; people tend to use the app more than they use the webpage for Facebook, as they do not necessarily need to log on via the internet on their laptops or PC; they go right to the app it's just easier to disseminate information, more accessible to add, friends, comment, respond and so on, it is then no surprise that 88% of all users use mobile now (66%) sixty-six percent of monthly mobile users use Facebook daily, so a lot of recurring users are going back on a day-to-day basis are two-thirds of the whole figure, so it's an addiction, and what Facebook offers is the opportunity to get information from the people you trust, care about and like to work with, you could also share a group with people you have a common interest with, you could also partake in the same organization, maybe have the same scheme, having the same group with the same passion, and that right there is what Facebook is, the commonality it establishes amongst people, and if you build up a network of that commonality, it is going to be addicting to take part in them. Facebook also bridges that gap between distance and sometimes the feeling of knowing that you are part of somebody's life daily by just being on Facebook is also part of what makes it addictive. Thinking further about it from an end user's perspective makes total sense. Now, if you wear your digital marketing thinking hat, you will be seeing this in the light of "Hey, two-thirds of a group of individuals or multiple users utilize it regularly, and there are billions of active users there."

Some of the things done on Facebook are posting polls, putting your Instagram feed in there, adding testimonials, getting creative, taking advantage of everything Facebook has to offer, and being true to yourself. Before you know it, you're going to start building up a community, gaining a reasonable amount of several likes on your business page, as well as some other tips. Now, for Facebook, when it comes to content you want to schedule your content, you don't want to just continue to post back-to-back you want to space your content out and another great advantage to Facebook as I already mentioned about social media marketing that's advertising so Facebook owns Instagram, they have an excellent tool for communicating called Facebook Messenger and so you can advertise leveraging Facebook messages you can leverage Instagram and what you need to do is if you go to Facebook's ad manager and you create a campaign when you go to create a campaign you are going click on placements and depending on what you are trying to do let us just say you are trying to build brand awareness you can actually hone in on you know Facebook you could hone in on Instagram you could do a number of different things within Facebook you have other ads available to you from single image ads to video ads to carousel see you have a lot of options and the most considerable opportunity on Facebook when it comes to advertising is your audience who are you targeting so remember Facebook has old young and everyone in between men and women and so you can specifically target interest you can specifically target gender and age allocation so Facebook really allows you to hone in on who your audience is if you're advertising and so that's the great thing about Facebook they have a lot of users and your you have an opportunity to hone in on a segment of that user base.

Manage your own media

Get educated now; don't get scared here. I'm not saying that you have to go to college and I'm not saying that you have to take my course. Getting educated can mean a variety of different things for different people. Still, I will say that one of the big things that I do see when people come to me to work with me as their coach is that they do not have an in-depth knowledge of what social media management is about. You need to know that it's essential to understand business and the business terms and the business processes. In addition to just knowing how to organically grow something, there are so many different ways to get educated; it doesn't have to be formal education necessarily.

Other Palace London — Social media!
YouTube - TRAILERS/REHEARSAL/MEET CAST
"Talks" - (Q&A)

Keep up to date on industry tools and technology;

Whether or not you want to pursue a formal education in marketing, you must keep up with the tools and tricks of the social media trade. Aside from the creative and community engagement aspects of social media, there is a science. To be successful, you must keep up with the analytics side of things and leverage the insights and data you gather to reach a wider audience. The most effective way to accomplish this is to stay current on the best and most popular social media management and social media marketing software options.

Look for social media opportunities wherever you go; Whatever role you are currently in, there is most likely a related opportunity to begin building your social media profile. Consult with your marketing team or company leadership to see if there is a way to promote your company's products or activities on social media. Also, don't be afraid to look for social media opportunities in your personal life. Encouraging your interests on Instagram may not unswervingly lead to your dream job, but it can add value to your resume and professional portfolio by demonstrating your ability to run a successful social media campaign.

Understand that you're constantly being watched; even if you're just operating a personal account, demonstrating a solid voice and consistent posting can help you get a foot in the door. This, however, works both ways. If you use poor judgment on public social media channels, it can and will be used against you.

Never cease to learn and adapt;

MySpace existed ten years ago. Snapchat has become popular in recent years. Because social media channels come and go, staying informed and adaptable is critical. This applies not only to channels but also to marketing disciplines.

You'll almost certainly need to have a thriving social media presence before you can sign up clients. Create accounts on all major social media platforms and become acquainted with blogging, email marketing, search engine optimization, and graphic design. You'll never be able to market for others if you can't market for yourself.

Even the most experienced social media marketing agencies struggle to find clients. Learn where your ideal potential clients spend their online time, distribute great content and start discussions to make money online.

Let's Talk Tips

Let us discuss some social media marketing tips for small businesses. I have outlined in this session how you can get more traffic to your website from social media. I have also outlined in this session how to get more engagement, and I have given a comprehensive explanation on how to get more followers and have also highlighted how to build your brand in a positive light so that people view your brand and then their trust grows in a significant way.

Now, the first thing you need to do is when you're creating your usernames use the same one, if possible, for all platforms; this means your username for Twitter should be the same for Facebook and should be the same for Instagram and Pinterest. If that is done, it'll make it easier for people to find you on social media

Remember to always have "follow" buttons on your website. If you have "follow" buttons on your website, it allows you to get the most followers possible by leveraging social media and leveraging the traffic from your website, and this is because you want to maximize the number of followers you have to get the most traffic.

You want to make a list of your competitors and industry leaders to study their patterns, so when you do this, and you actually study the people that are the best in your industry, you'll notice that you can find patterns in what they're doing you can find consistent things that multiple brands that are leaders in their industry do that you can incorporate into your business. If you go to twitter.com, you can create a list from your profile of profiles that you want to follow and that you want to observe. You should always be learning from the best as you go on. You should always observe who is doing something well that you want to do well to get the best tools and strategies to get you there.

You need to post daily; the more you post, the better in some cases, but you need to post at least once a day on every single platform; that's one thing you cannot afford to not do. You have to post daily; this will ensure an excellent infographic structure or system in place. You don't want to post any more than twice a day on Facebook because the shelf life of a Facebook post is much longer than, say, Pinterest or Twitter; in other words, it stays in the newsfeed longer on Facebook than it does others. All you need to do is understand the psychology behind and the numbers behind posting, how many different times per day, and why it works. Don't over-post and don't under post

Use easy social share buttons for WordPress. This is a plug-in, which applies if you have a WordPress website. If you don't have a

WordPress website, you might find a different alternative. But WordPress has one of those great options that most social media share buttons don't have, as it allows you to follow somebody after you share their content. So, it naturally gets you many more followers from people already sharing stuff you must have posted before.

Use a scheduler like Buffer or HootSuite. Now, HootSuite allows you to put all your private messages from social media in one dashboard so you can view all of them on one screen; it also allows you to automate posting so you can create a schedule and every time you upload a post into that, it will post it on that schedule automatically for you. Buffer does a lot of the same stuff; they don't have the messaging thing, but they also have West branding, so it just kind of depends on what you're looking for; they both have free plans so you could try out any. You might even find a way to use both of them at the same time. You can always use one of two apps to automate social media a little bit and just make it to where you don't have to keep logging back on just to post every single time.

Studying analytics to find popular trends. Here, you're looking for the popularity of posts; you're looking out for indicators of what posts are working and what posts are not. There are actually a lot of great analytic tools for social media because social media is so popular. Keyhole has a great post called the list of the top 25 social media analytics tools. That is going to be a great list that will show you different tools and what they do to give you an idea of what you'll need, but then, because everybody has their own needs, you need to be studying the numbers from social media because if you don't know the numbers, you won't know how to stop doing what's not working and stop wasting your time and you won't know how to build on things that are working because you won't know which ones are. You won't know which posts are getting the most engagement. So, if you have a post that gets you 50 shares and a post that gets zero, you need to stop doing the types of posts that get zero and build on the ones that get 50 shares. You build your brand more over time by working more efficiently, and to work more efficiently, you need analytics.

Show a little humanity and be relatable. The human side of social media is one of the most powerful strategies. Social media will constantly be changing; it will continuously be improving. Different apps will pop up, different services will pop up, but the same principles will apply. Principles like being human on social media and showing that you're not just a robot, you're not just completely automating everything, you're actually caring about what people are interacting with, you care about responding to their messages.

Make your profile look professional and inviting. Showcase your credibility indicators. Things like these can really earn people's trust before they even know who you are. If you prove that you are trustworthy and credible in your industry, they will trust you more and even thank you more. Putting yourself out with strategic details will build trust with people. Share your accomplishments, share your education your certifications and make a professional profile don't look like an amateur

Interact with your followers. You want to interact with your followers. If you do not, it's going to be too one-sided. Engage with people. Show them that you're reading what they're writing. Giving a personal touch on social media does not give the impression that makes them feel that you are a robot and just posting stuff without actually responding to anyone. The whole idea is that you want to respond to people, join chats, ask followers questions, let them know your opinions, retweet them back, and share the post that you think was really intriguing. This kind of action can help build your brand and really make people like you because they'll see that you're actually paying attention to them and giving them respect and attention

Remember, Facebook Loves Facebook. As a small business, you're probably going to have a Facebook page, one of the leading social media platforms out there. If you have a Facebook page. Now, let us talk about some posts on Facebook and how they work. For instance, when you post content, say a video, and upload it directly to Facebook as a Facebook video and not a YouTube video, you will notice that there will be a lot of engagement. If you compare that to content posted as a link to maybe a video on YouTube, it gets a lot less engagement. So, Facebook loves Facebook. They want you to stay on Facebook; they don't want you to go through links or go to other websites; they want you to stay on Facebook as long as possible. So don't share YouTube videos on Facebook; upload the video directly to Facebook. Don't share a lot of links. Share images. Do things that will get engagement but still keep them on Facebook's website.

Put yourself in your follower's shoes. Think about what they are looking at, put yourself in their position; how would you feel if you showed another brand post what you just posted. It is believed that people don't ever think from the other person's perspective. If you did, you might understand some more. If you cannot figure out why they're not engaging with your profile or why they are not following you on social media, then there's a reason for it, there's an excellent reason for it, you have to just figure it out by putting yourself in their shoes. You can even go to a consumer testing website, where you can test websites and social media profiles and products and things like that to figure out what you're doing right and what you're doing wrong and get other people's perspectives. When you post it, look at your own stuff and figure out how you would feel about it if you weren't a part of the company, or just ask your family and friends or ask people you don't know or ask employees what they think.

80% value 20% percent promotions. Keep this in mind; the 80/20 rule is essential for not driving away all your followers. What you do here is; you post value entertaining, educational type stuff 80% of the time, and then you do promotions for your brand 20% of the time if you do promotions for your brand like coupons and sales and all that stuff all the time people are going to get bored. The point is, they don't care about your advertisements unless they already like your brand, so to get people to like your brand, you need to post things like videos, behind-the-scenes photos, educational stuff, quotes, images of some of your employees having a lot of fun with customers. Always provide value with nothing in return and 20% selling or promoting.

Maximize reach with post timings. Your timing needs to be great; you need to keep this in mind all the time. Post at the correct times, on the right platforms. Different platforms require different posting times. For instance, on Facebook, you look at 9 a.m., 1 p.m., and 3 p.m. For Twitter, 12:00 p.m., 3 p.m., 5 & 6 p.m. Wednesday is the best day to post.

Only use platforms that make sense. Just because there are a few dozen social media platforms doesn't mean you should use every one of them. Just because one brand uses it doesn't mean you should. You shouldn't just be a jack of all social media platforms; you should master just those that will get you more business. It will waste time if it doesn't benefit you and your customer base. Don't waste any time. Work as efficiently as possible on social media

Mix up content mediums. In other words, use photos, words, quotes, videos, infographics, questions, polls. There are a lot of different types of posts that you can do. The idea is to master the art of mixing up your content on social media.

People should not be able to predict what you will post next. Keep them on their toes, and keep them wanting more.

Link your website to all your profiles. This is very important because you're not getting all your business just on your social media profiles. Link your website from all your profiles to get more traffic, get more subscribers to your mailing list, and get more customers trying to get quotes and things like that on your website.

Brand your images and your videos. When you post videos and images, which are some of the most popular ways to get more engagement on social media, you'll notice that branding can really help you. Now, for instance, if you're on Facebook and you share a post on Facebook like I highlighted earlier, you don't want to post a lot of links here, and this is because you'll get a minimal amount of reach of your followers as very few of your followers will actually see links that you post on your page, so it's better to post more images.

We have established that Facebook gives more engagement to posts directly on Facebook and gives less attention to links that lead to other websites. If you study Facebook posts very well, you'll notice there's always a trend of images and directly uploaded videos getting more engagement on Facebook than links leading to other websites. Therefore, you want to do those things. But when you share an image, Now, say you share an image, and there's no link to your profile on the image, people are not going to know much about who the post is from, or let's say they share the image or they save it and post it somewhere else, if you have your logo at the bottom, you will get more people visiting without even having to have a direct link. So, just get your brand in front of as many people as possible, and it is also like a sign. If you go down a street and you do not see a sign for a business like a restaurant or something, maybe there's no direct link, then it's just a place, with no direction or information leading to where it is, but when you can see the brand sign up or down the road even before getting to the location of the business, it gives you a sense of direction. It is the same on social media. Your brand allows people on social media to see who it's from the source of the image. It also makes your image look more professional because the logo always looks good. So, when people share your images and share videos without a direct link, make sure you have your logo on it.

Now, you need to know why people actually engage with things on social media. There's a psychology to it, and there are five main reasons people share content on social media. According to neuroscience, they share it to entertain, inspire, or be useful most times. When people share your post instead of just like it, they share it because they want their friends to see it, and if their friends see it, they feel good about being connected to that post. So, make your post shareable. Make it look good when people share it because it's positive, motivating, entertaining, and engaging. Another thing in psychology is; we share to express who we really are. So, if people resonate with something that you post a lot of times, they'll share it. Community to nurture your relationship. So, you could share it to say they might feel like it helps them connect with people or help them develop a connection with their friends that they haven't talked to in a long time. Motivation is another thing. Quotes get shared a lot if there are quotes because they're motivating. The quote motivates them, and this means it might motivate their friends too.

Let us dive deeper into this. Taking more advanced steps forward;

Find out where your ideal clients hang out. Where are they? Are they on Linkedin? If you're selling B to B, I think Linkedin is a compelling platform because many businesses are on Linkedin. If you're selling B to C, business to consumer, then maybe Instagram is the way to go, Facebook is the way to go, or YouTube is the way to go, Snapchat or Twitter. Whatever it is that you choose. But you want to be very, very clear who your ideal customers are. Who are your ideal prospects, and where do they hang out? Where are they out of this vast ocean of the internet and this information highway? Where do they spend their time? Figure out first, where are they hanging out? Find out, where are they?

Secondly, You want to get in front of them; you want to just pick one out of all these platforms. One of the worst things you can do is get on all these platforms. You've got your Twitter, your Facebook, your YouTube, your Instagram, you got your Linkedin, you try to do them all. When you try to do that, you will fail, a hundred percent, because each channel, each platform has its own uniqueness. You need to market to the audience very differently. The way you talk to them is very different. Unless, like me, you've grown to the point where you have a pretty big team to do all these things when you're just getting started. Just pick one. Maybe it's YouTube, Instagram, or Linkedin. Just pick one platform. And you focus on that platform, and you focus on just mastering and understanding that platform. And you learn everything you possibly could about that one platform.

As you do your marketing, you create content, add value, learn, and get feedback on where the strategy is working in the marketplace. Then you can improve from there. Every single course, let's say you want to learn about Instagram, you want to master Instagram, you want to market on Instagram. Get every course that you can. Read every book that you could on just that, on Instagram. And you master that. And implement the ideas. And you go back and implement. You reflect, learn from it, and you implement. That's how you get going with social media marketing. Don't try to do them all, right? Jack of all trades, master of none.

You sell them something. What? That's right. You fucking sell them something. You need to sell something in exchange for money. You can't just have social media following and hope that someday that will turn into money. I have a friend of mine. I won't name any names. She's a top, one of the top ten influencers in Canada, on social media, top ten, like (claps hands) magazines feature her, like top ten in terms of influence. She's broke, making less than $30,000 a year. Looks glamorous; it looks like there are a lot of followers; you can't make money. And when I was talking to her in private, and she was crying, and she's like, "I've been doing this, I've been creating content, and people think I'm so successful. I've got this massive social media following. I can't even pay my rent." I asked when the last time you sold something to your audience was? She said, "Well, I don't want to sell anything to my audience. They would think that I'm a sellout. I don't know if I should sell something. I can't talk about that. I'm gonna lose my audience." That is the wrong attitude. The only purpose of being on social media is to bring in business. Some people use social media for pleasure; I think poor people break people and use social media for pleasure. I use social media for profit. I'm not on social media for pleasure. I am on social media to make a profit, grow my company, and build my brand. That's the only sane reason to be on social media. As a byproduct of that, I get to impact millions of people. But I don't lose focus because I'm using social media as a tool, as a vehicle to grow my company, period, period. So you need to think about that. What is your intent, what is your outcome? You need to be clear that you're out there. You've got to sell them something. If you cannot overcome that, you have a problem with selling. You'll always struggle with making money on social media.

Chapter One
LinkedIn Strategy

Now let us talk LinkedIn. This is a subject matter that I have always loved to write about, and it's one that many of you will be happy to learn from as you go through the material.

Now let's make our knowledge more concrete. You might still feel unsure or uncertain of what to post for your business on LinkedIn. Let us review some top strategies for post types best utilized on LinkedIn. Now LinkedIn is quite different from other platforms, and your ability to see it through this lens goes a long way. Think about it in comparison to other social media platforms out there. Let's compare Facebook, Instagram, and LinkedIn regarding how you post your content. Facebook has an energy that has self-eye focus. We tend to use the word "I did this," "This happened to me," and it has very self-interested energy. And on Instagram, it has that "us-you-energy." When you think about influencers on Instagram, they want you to click on the product. They want you to know what they're up to. LinkedIn has a we-energy. We want to be spoken with. When you're creating posts and content inside LinkedIn, it's a collective team, peer energy voice. So think about your colleagues and your peers and how you would speak with them, and that's the type of energy we want to see in a LinkedIn post

The LinkedIn Strategy

We are going to go over the best LinkedIn marketing strategy. I have strategically outlined an eight-step plan in chronological order and the most important things you need to consider when implementing a LinkedIn marketing strategy. Now, when you first implement a strategy on LinkedIn, the number one question you need to ask yourself is "Who?". Who do you want to reach? Who is your audience?, Who is a potential consumer of your product?. Having answers to these questions will give a deeper insight into the steps we discuss. Now let's talk about these steps.

Know your audience

who is your avatar? What do they look like on surface level? in terms of geographical location, where are they based, what kind of companies do they belong to? is it a solo entrepreneur? is it a fortune 500 company? These questions will reveal a thing that is not just on the surface level; they go in-depth to dig up the emotional level. You need to understand the people you're selling to, what keeps them up at night, what drives them, what they are most afraid of, and what they are trying to achieve? What will that achievement mean for their personal lives? Now you have to focus on two different levels of understanding;

The surface level and then the emotional level. You want to make sure that you do that work before you even look at any social media strategy on any platform. You need to know who you're marketing to; otherwise, all your efforts are going to be void, and it's just going to be luck whether or not it works.

Optimize your profile

When potential clients come to your profile page or are just there to look, your profile answers three questions, which is really important. When a user comes to your LinkedIn profile, they are subconsciously not aware of it, but they're looking to answer three questions to themselves as fast as possible, and those three questions are

Is this a valuable person to me?

Is this person credible? social proof is where that comes in big time

Is interacting with this person valuable and beneficial to me?

Right now, with a timing sense of urgency, you can answer those three questions through how you layout your profile, then you are onto a winner. Your profile doesn't necessarily need to be or look like a CV. It is a landing page. You have a purpose for it. The kind of conversion you want to gain from somebody who goes onto your profile will determine how you'd lay it out. Do you want them to message you? Do you want them to go to your website? Do you want them to read a blog post? you need to set it up in a way that asks for that response

Grow your network.

Now, when you grow your network grows it bearing two different types of people in mind;

Thought leaders. These could be direct competitors. These could be indirect competitors just in a public space you are interested in.

Clients. These are people you see as ideal prospects, people you want to bring into your network so they can be exposed to your content, which I will be shedding more light on as we move on together. This set of people will come to you inbound most often, even when it's not the right time. They might never approach you on their own. If you approach them outbound, they might not convert, but if they do, have it at the back of your mind that that is an ideal kind of client and that they can be pre-qualified to an extent.

You can also grow using the accessible version of LinkedIn, or you can grow using sales navigation which I'll go into a little more as we move on.

Implement a content strategy

This is so important, it used to be a lot easier to grow on LinkedIn as the organic reach used to be insane, but since LinkedIn has advertising capabilities and now to get more and more spread in any platform, usage of ads are the way forward, as it is harder to get organic growth, but it's not impossible. You have to think about who you're creating your content for when it comes to content.

Out-bounding selling

Now let us address the issue of inbound versus outbound. Inbound is people coming to us. This mainly comes from content and word of mouth referrals and stuff like that, and then outbound is when you're going out and chasing that bread, it's that you're going out, you're going to approach that person, it is you reaching out to them the main thing to bear in mind when it comes to outbound is that it is a fast-selling method. This is the future and what everybody is into; personalization, putting the buyer first, the virtual direction in which sales are heading, and more importantly, is set in place. Outbound, you must realize that you anticipate a personalized answer if you deliver a tailored message to a potential customer. You need to genuinely want to connect with them as human beings; you need to constantly give off the energy to treat them as a person, not as a sales opportunity, essential for outbound.

Referral scheme

Now, this is the one you're probably like, oh, I didn't expect you to throw that in there. Many of the people I lectured and taught when I first started giving out relevant and valuable information to business owners with clients always talked about generating new leads generating new businesses. My question has always been, "what about a current business that you have and current opportunities that you maybe haven't explored yet?". You seem to want to knock on different doors and see which ones open. When it comes to referral schemes, are there happy clients? Clients that you currently work with or that you have worked with in the past that you haven't said: "hey, hello, err… I've got my trail of thought that you haven't reached out to, and I just wanted to ask if you know anybody that would actually be a perfect fit for my services". The thing is this, most of the time, happy clients will do this by themselves, but if you haven't asked, then ask them, and even have an incentive to set up a referral scheme where you say, "Oh, to any of you that refer me a client which I end up signing up, I'll give you a 30% commission on the first month of us working together or a 10% recurring commission every single month for as long as they stay". You need to come up with a referral scheme and an incentive, and that will work as an excellent way for current businesses to continue generating new companies in the background while you also work on your outbound marketing strategy. The referral scheme is super important.

Implement CRM (Customer Relationship Management)

You should learn this; you don't have to do it the hard way. It is more straightforward and essential; you pay attention to where the money is coming from and make sure it stays open. You let that client know that "I SEE YOU" to them. It might not look like that, but you know what you are doing and working on when you call and send the emails. Now, if you ignore the implementation of the CRM and stop tracking your customers on both the front end and back end, you will affect inflow. You would begin to see the effect on your money inflow. You would notice that you are not pulling in as much money. So, get a CRM. It doesn't have to be pricey. You can use a spreadsheet. It can be free also as you can use something like pipe-drive, I think zopto is another one, and there are so many options available in the market, so take a look; you could use a spreadsheet at most and track your conversions. If you don't follow them, you cannot optimize, and this right here is the 101. You could also think of it as a scientific experiment.

Split test and optimize

Now, once you've been using one set of messaging or one type of content you want to take a look at your numbers from that, you want to note them down and say, okay, when I send out 100 messages saying this, I get this many acceptances, this many people accept, many people positively respond to me, this amount of people convert into a meeting, and these many people close. Once you have that information, you can say, "Okay, what happens if I change this variable about the messaging "Do the same thing happen? Track the numbers. Where do you see a higher close rate at the back end, and then you can do the same thing for different marketing elements, so you can do that for messaging? You can also do that for content. You could do a split-test video versus a photo. Use split-test photo versus text. You could split-test photo versus carousel, there are so many different ways you can mix and match, and it's kind of like systemic testing if you were doing Facebook ads or like paid traffic. You could do the same thing for your organic marketing methods as well.

The LinkedIn Prospect

Going further, let us begin to dig this up from a different angle. Another solid tip that I can give you to impact your LinkedIn content strategy is that instead of thinking of LinkedIn as a professional place to put content, replace the word professional with leadership. Create a container of leadership voice that is peer-related, and you will have a very successful content strategy. Let's start high-level and think of several content strategy categories that you can lump your content into, and then we'll get into more specifics.

Industry insights.

The best way to think about industry insights is relevant news in your industry, but you share your different opinion as a company or a brand. Another example of an industry insight is all pertinent conferences or Events or podcasts you recently listened to that you're able to share as a post.

Storytelling.

We want to see some behind the scenes of your business, we want to get access to your team and what is happening, and we also love hearing your experiences and stories. Share the action-oriented type of posts, showing the before and after, or a team that is attending a conference.

Be relatable.

What I mean by that is sharing things that are either humorous in ways that we can relate to you through the books you're reading or podcasts you're listening to. We must recognize each category as a human element, which is the most critical takeaway from each category. Your viewers want access to your thoughts and insights on current articles and news. They want access to your team and stories and what is happening, and lessons learned through your business.

The LinkedIn Prospect II

Now, let's share a quick post formula that you can plug all of your LinkedIn content.

"Open up with a hook."

It is a value-based statement and what that means is that the audience knows why this post will matter to them.

Now, the following part of the content formula is the intriguing line. The goal is to get people to click on the *"See More"* button to expand the entire post. In that intriguing line, we want to know the content that can reveal more to spark inquisitiveness in the ears of the user. If you are about to tell us a story, give us something relatable, or give us your insights into a news topic.

The last part of the formula is the juiciest. Give people a call to action. You have earned the right to that call to action. What I mean by that is you've given us the value; you have told us what we are about to get in the intrigue. You deliver it, and then you provide us with something to do. Either that means booking a call or directing people to click on one of the buttons you created above on your company page.

One bonus tip is to use that call to action to match the language you used in the short tagline that you created for your company page. For example, "If you want to check out the full LinkedIn company page and how to create that tagline, we're going to link that in the description below."

LinkedIn Contentology

Now, you have the language you're going to use. You have the categories that work the best and the post formula. So let's get into the content types.

This first content type is something that most people do not think about, but I'm going to give it away to you; commenting. I want to clarify that you can comment in the newsfeed as a company page as your company brand. That is something that many people do not realize and don't take advantage of. The easiest way to engage on the platform and comment is to first reply to comments already happening on your content. The next best place for your company to comment is to engage and respond to people already tagging your brand and your company in their posts. The final easiest way to comment as a brand is to go out in those community hashtags where your content is already trending and continue to pop up and get visibility for your company brand within those three community hashtags generated.

The second content type is "shares." When you share content on LinkedIn, it gets more visibility when you add your own opinion. That is the value that your ideal client wants to follow and engage with on your company page. Another great way to think about LinkedIn content sharing to your company page is to go out and see what your team is creating on their profiles as content. For example, if you have a CEO or even an intern making content on their profile on LinkedIn.

The third one is text-only posts. On LinkedIn, texts are only three lines. The text-only post has five lines, and then you can open up the rest of the post. So that is the only difference I wanted to point out between text-only and all the rest of the posts on LinkedIn. We have an image with a text post, then show authentic photos instead of stock photos. We want to connect with you and your brand, and you should take advantage of that by sharing authentic images with your branding.

External links, news features, blog posts, and YouTube videos are the following content type. LinkedIn is different from other social media sites. They will push content out to external links, and that is a powerful content strategy to drive traffic from your LinkedIn company page to an external source.

The fourth content type is the document feature. This one is relatively new to LinkedIn, and it is powerful. When somebody checks out your past posts, it has its featured newsfeed just for documents. The other unique thing about documents is that they are swipe-able visual files. What that means for you is that it starts to preview the image of the next slide, which creates intrigue for people to want to see what is next. You may see this as a slidable feature or a carousel-type post on other social media platforms. It is the same thing. The most significant difference is that it's uploaded as either a PDF, a word document, or a PowerPoint slide deck.

The fifth content strategy type is video. I get excited about a video because that is the fastest way to connect visually with your customers and get clients. Plus, video on LinkedIn is still undersaturated. Keep the videos short, either a minute to two minutes long, and we want to see that there will be people in this video. We want access to who is behind the scenes working on those products or services, even if it's a product or service. Merge the LinkedIn video with either readable content or captions. That way, we can watch the video on silent, and you can get more attention from your potential customers or clients who may be consuming your video at their place of work.

The sixth "content-type" is LinkedIn live video. The number one thing you want to be aware of with LinkedIn live is that it does require an application to get access and a third-party tool to go live on the platform. You can go live spontaneously. You can schedule your life in advance and go live within an event, which creates a chat feature that allows your audience to connect. When somebody opens up your LinkedIn profile, instead of seeing your LinkedIn banner at the top, they will be able to watch you like a TV screen from your LinkedIn profile. It will be the live video playing there. Since people can land on your profile over and over again, you can create a consistent schedule for your LinkedIn lives and direct them to the same link every single time. As of this recording and depending on your third-party tool, the ability to have your banner image turn into the LinkedIn live video is currently only available on the personal LinkedIn profile, but It is anticipated that it might roll out to the LinkedIn company pages.

The next hot new feature for LinkedIn is LinkedIn polls. It is a great tool to use for audience research and marketing questions. Click to start a post. Hover over the image of a survey. It says Create a poll. You open up with a question, and you have four choices your audience can choose. And the poll duration, you can choose from one day, three days, one week, or two weeks. I recommend that works the best is one week of poll duration. That way, you get people to engage in the conversation in the comments. An excellent strategy for polls is to keep it simple. The best way to keep it simple is to have the question in the text post, a call to action to vote, the same question in the poll, and then give people three options, with the fourth option to be other, comment below.

The eighth "content-type" is articles. It is the only type of content on LinkedIn that encourages you to tweet and share them over to Facebook. The key to getting more visibility on your LinkedIn article is to optimize the image. A LinkedIn article has solid potential, when optimized, to go highly viral outside of LinkedIn, and that is probably the top piece of content that can do that on LinkedIn.

The ninth "content-type" is LinkedIn stories. It is a relatively new feature, and It's mainly accessible from your mobile device. Twenty seconds long, you get three ways to drive traffic from a LinkedIn story.

The first one, just by having a company page. You automatically get swiped up on your LinkedIn company stories no matter how many followers. On your profile, then the swipe-up feature is only available to you if you have 5,000 followers and your Follow button is the primary button instead of Connect. At the bottom of every LinkedIn, the story is to reply to that story. On the company page, you cannot exchange messages through LinkedIn stories.

That's why the second option I'm about to give you is essential for company pages. You want to encourage people to click on the image in the upper left-hand corner, the company logo you have uploaded for your company page. That gives them direct access to open up your profile or company page.

And the final LinkedIn content type is LinkedIn events. The way you get access to it is to go to your home page at the top, where you say Add a post. It has the option to click event. You get access to create an event, either as yourself or as a company page. The most potent parts of LinkedIn events are the cover image and logo that goes with the event. My best tip for you is to show people. If people are speaking at your event, showcase their photos, make sure to highlight those attending your event already as a speaker or attendee. Another business advantage to LinkedIn events is creating an opt-in link when you start the event. Every person registering for a LinkedIn event is also added to your email list. A great way to get the word out about your event is the ability to invite attendees from your current audience. You can also create a filter to invite the specific, ideal client to attend this event.

Now let me give an example of a solid post type that is text-only; that you can make within five minutes that gets excellent engagement and response. Announce to the platform that you're getting more active here on LinkedIn, either as your profile or your company page. Ask for advice for whom you should connect with or follow or engage with on the platform; then, pick hashtags where you think your ideal client is currently pursuing. That is a powerful post for LinkedIn because it encourages tagging and engagement and introduces you to new people you may not have connected with before. All of the content types we just covered can get even more reach when paired with a great hashtag strategy.

Chapter Two
Instagram Marketing

Let us now discuss marketing strategies, concepts, and principles that work for Instagram. Instagram is a social media platform that needs no introduction with nearly 1 billion monthly active users and 500 million daily active users. Instagram is a platform drive with marketing potential; Instagram mobile generates more than 7 billion in revenue, and it is home to more than two million advertisers; not only that, marketing on Instagram has the following advantages. You have increased conversions according to research; more than one-third of the people using the app have used it to purchase products which mean by marketing your products on the app, there's a higher chance of conversion, you also have advanced targeting options, and this is, in fact, thanks to Instagram's parent company Facebook. Instagram has access to just about all advertising features offered by Facebook ads; with this, you can advertise to people based on their age, location, gender interests, and much more; you can also build better brand follower relationships; you can stimulate conversion with your followers and build a connection with them. You'll also get a greater understanding of what your followers like and dislike based on their engagement; this enables you to make the content they enjoy more and increase the chance of converting a user to a consumer.

Instagram marketing.

Now, let's look at how marketing is done on Instagram. Let us start with number one

Your bio is the first thing people notice when they get to your page. That is where customers establish their first impression of your brand; therefore, your bio should contain information, fascinating and engaging. Your bio should include a brief description of your company or product, the sort of material you want to share, brand hashtags, connections to other social media sites, and additional information. Your bio should also include a URL to where you want people to go, whether it's your brand's website or a page for a specific product; track this link as well to see how much traffic it delivers.

Now, when your audience is engaged, a calendar allows you to decide what content, captions, hashtags, and videos go live on what day, date, or time; a consistent post schedule enables you to make the most of Instagram; it will also keep your audience engaged and provide you with access to historical posts.

Now, you can keep track of your postings using content calendars. It will also let you plan and automate the publication of your content. We need to create a content calendar. If you ask anyone who works with social media, one of the most important things they will tell you is to have a content calendar.

Shown below is an example of a template.

Ads options are pretty similar to what you have on Facebook. You can now segment your audience based on their likes, interactions, purchasing patterns, and more; you also have several ad styles to select from, such as story advertising, picture advertisements, video ads, collection ads, and more; and you can also put them up from Facebook ads management. Here's an example of Bodyshop advertising in which they use a single picture ad. The advertisement is effective because of its engaging creative, and appealing ad language, enticing customers to connect with the post and click on the link.

You can get greater reach with ads. Paid ads can enable you to get more followers. Engagement leads and conversions, the caveat here being that you'll need to pay for it too.

Having a visually consistent feed on IG is a process that builds up feedback over time. Instagram is a platform where people gravitate towards aesthetically pleasing content, authentic expressions, and diverse perspectives. The objective is that your feed needs to match your brand's identity and appeal to your industry's audience. What works nowadays are candid shots muted earthly tones with a low-key editing style. Your content must feel down-to-earth and your brand approachable.

Always try to tell a story about whatever content you post. The images, videos, and stories you post must tell stories that captivate your audience and connect with them; this increases the likelihood that they will feel closer to your brand and purchase your products; your captions can tell stories that help your brand appear more human and build deeper connections with your audience. Your content should align with what your audience cares about or solve problems they face. Here's an example of how Patagonia's page talks about forests in America. Their posts tell a different story about a separate issue that affects nature. Their brand on Instagram revolves around bringing awareness to such matters.

Using the right hashtags can make the difference between your posts showing up on the explore tab for everyone to see, and it is getting lost in the sea of content. Your hashtags shouldn't be too generic like new year or hash style since they'll have too much competition; instead, mix up trending. Industry-specific keywords to connect with your follower's research on successful hashtags and limit yourself to less than seven in each post. The more the hashtags in your post, the more likely it seems spammy untargeted, and unprofessional to find out what and how many hashtags your competitors use and how you can do something similar you could also create a hashtag for your brand; these need to be short easily memorable and involve your brand name in some way.

Using UGC or user-generated content allows your followers to become more involved with your brand. You can convert followers into your brand advocates using UGC, regardless of the field your brand belongs to. Here's an example of how Starbucks uses user-generated content and takes advantage of their audience to advertise their products; in this post here, they are attracting customers with an image of happy children dressed in

Taking advantage of video ads, most Instagramers state that users have visited their websites and searched or told a friend after being influenced by posts; even though photo ads are still the more popular form of advertising, video advertisements aren't too far behind there are three key video formats when it comes to Instagram ads single video ads that can create 60-second ads carousels are a combination of images and videos and Instagram stories that enable you to combine images and videos to create visually attractive ads here's an example of the brand pizza 73 using story ads to advertise their pizzas it's successful because you're showing off the product they are promoting with well short videos and captions

Partner up with influencers. Connecting with influencers will enable you to connect with thought leaders within the industry and show off your brand to a larger audience by clicking with them. Your brand will have greater authenticity and authority. Influencers need new tools, resources, and guidance to effectively carry out their role and work together as partners. Consider Micro-influencers as they are more affordable and closer to their audience. We can see how Ralph Lauren has collaborated with an influencer to advertise its products. The influencer showing off the latest ralph Lauren has to offer encourages his interested followers to check out the page and buy something for themselves.

Host contests and giveaways as much as you can. Competitions allow your audience to interact with your business by receiving 3.5 times the number of likes and 64 times the number of comments. You may offer a product or service to increase engagement and brand exposure: planning contests, partnering with brands, Identifying contest rules, and much more. Monitoring the competition and then running it is also very important. You need to track your contest performance and promote the results on other social media platforms.

Using stories and IGTv stories allows you to create a combination of photos and videos that disappear after 24 hours. This, in the long run, can significantly influence your reach and engagement rates, even giving your account the chance to show up in the explore section it can also help make your brand seem more approachable and authentic adding links to the Instagram stories can also help with driving traffic to your website.

Track and learn to identify effective hashtags, visual styles, and the best times to post doing this, and you can develop the best practices for your brand. Social listening and analytics will help you fine-tune your marketing strategy and increase Instagram engagement.

Tools and apps

We also need to understand that growing an Instagram account takes a lot of time and energy, and you might need the help of tools to achieve this. While running Instagram ads and reaching out to influencers is highly effective, there are specific tools that you can use to turbocharge your Instagram account. This book will offer several applications and technologies to supplement your growth plan. You'll discover how to expand your reach, save time, develop a brand look and feel, drive more consumers to your online business, and boost loyalty with your current audience.

Now let us discuss these apps and tools to help you level up your Instagram game and set you apart from the others.

Trufan.

With this app, you can discover highly engaged followers and engage them even further to turn them into brand advocates. Basically, with Trufan, you can strengthen these relationships and encourage them to proactively share about your brand via social and word of mouth. Trufan is more than just an Instagram growth tool, and it's a business growth tool that increases fan loyalty and ambassadorship.

Adobe rush.

Rush allows you to edit your videos directly on your phone. It mimics Adobe premiere if you're familiar with that, but it makes it so much easier. It simplifies the process. So even if you're a beginner, you can create captivating videos super quickly, and they even have to format your videos for stories or feed posts. You also get three video exports to start for free.

Display purposes.

This web-based tool delivers all the details that you need to know regarding Instagram hashtags. One of my favorite things about this tool is seeing related hashtags. If your goal is to grow on Instagram using hashtags, then this tool will help spark some ideas for new hashtags while still ensuring that you're hitting your target audience.

Instagram analytics.

Now the thing is this, you might've overlooked Instagram's in-app analytics, but it is a powerhouse. Basically, at just a glance, you can see who your audience is, what kind of content resonates with them, and you can see your growth over time. Using this tool can better cater to your current and desired audience, setting you up for development. So, for example, if you've identified that most of your audience is based in Brooklyn, you might want to create content that connects with a Brooklyn subculture, which will help you expand your growth within that niche.

Gleam.io.

It is widely known that running contests can grow your Instagram account quickly, and with Gleam, you can run tournaments, track entries, pick winners, showcase user submissions, and a lot more. This tool is super powerful, and it makes entries a lot more seamless than other apps. Seamless entries will result in higher conversions and more followers for your brand.

Big Vu.

If you're a small business owner, you understand the importance of personal connection with your audience on Instagram because it increases engagement. Get on camera and chat with your followers as if they were your friends. It will build community, but not everyone is comfortable; not everyone is a pro when putting yourself online. So that being said, Big VU is a teleprompter app that will help you script and shoot your videos so that you can speak on camera, like a confident pro. It's also going to automatically transcribe your words into captions, which makes your videos more inclusive and more of an engaging experience.

Mention-Lytics

This tool tracks the mentions of your brand so that you can identify where your brand is being mentioned most. You're going to want to use that data to understand what content resonates with people. And then once you have a firm grasp on that, you're going to be able to make more content just like that, to continue the buzz and keep that conversation going. This will help with engagement, help exposure, and help with your follower account.

Canva.

Canva is a free web-based graphic design platform where you can easily layout professional-looking content. You can design with graphics animations, you can create with texts, and you can use your original photos, or you have the option of using stock photography. You don't need a degree in design to use this. And even if you're not a hundred percent comfortable with technology, Canva makes it so easy to communicate product drops visually. Maybe you have some quotes you want to put on your Instagram. You can lay out some company news or sale events. Whatever it is that you're looking for, Canva makes it easy. I would recommend you use this tool where appropriate, though, because when you're on Instagram, most users are looking for organic content. Sometimes when you over-design, this tends to lose engagement, so make sure that you're just saving this tool for infographics, or even if you want to put your logo in your profile picture, this is a fantastic tool for that as well.

HootSuite.

HootSuite is a scheduling tool that takes a lot of that grunt work out of posting to Instagram. Images, videos, and stories can be mailed directly from HootSuite, whether you're on a desktop or whether you're on mobile. On this tool, you can dedicate a few hours a month, at the beginning of the month, to scheduling all your content out at once and then not having to think about doing that later. This tool is excellent for growth because it keeps you on track for posting content consistently. And we all know that consistent material is impressive for growing an Instagram account.

Vsco

Vsco is an app that is best known for its filters. Ten of which are completely free when you download the app. So, if you're looking to tighten up your branding, sticking with one or two Vsco filters and applying that to your entire grid will help you develop your brand, look and feel, and more consistency throughout your grid. Whether your brand aesthetic is grunge or whether you're more of the soft and straightforward type, Vsco can help develop that tone and better relate to your desired audience. Having a consistent brand look and feel will help boost the engagement, and it's going to help boost your follower account when it comes to building a brand Instagram profile.

Prequel.

Let us compare these apps in the same field. The Vsco app also offers filters, but the prequel app is trendier, and they're bolder. These are going to be especially useful if you're appealing to gen Z. So, while prequel is not going to gain you more followers directly, this tool is going to help you send visual cues that you are on-trend, and we've come to learn that visual cues are essential to gen

Z, an audience that is highly literate in visual aesthetic. So, if you're marketing to gen Z, the prequel app can be an excellent tool for you.

Keyhole.

Are you using branded hashtags? If you are a keyhole, you can calculate the ROI of your branded hashtags. And if you're working with influencers, Keyhole will also measure if your influencers have successfully used your branded hashtags. Preview, this feed planning app helps you curate a visually cohesive feed. So, you can move your photos around where they look best, and you can schedule them in time for your brand campaigns. It also helps plan your captions, and you can copy-paste and save hashtags.

Dovetale.

If influencer marketing is part of your growth strategy, Dovetale is a fantastic platform to help you find those niche influencers on Instagram. So, you can search by keyword. You can search by location, engagement rate, and the number of followers with this tool. Dovetale helps ensure that your influencer campaigns show a return on investment by starting with the right fit. Brand collabs manager. Dovetale can tend to be a little pricey, so if you're looking for a budget-friendly alternative, Instagram business and creator accounts now have access to Facebook's brand collabs manager. This platform is designed to make it easy for compatible brands and influencers to find each other and collaborate on campaigns. Brands can look up lists of creators based on their past partner creators who liked their account and set up audience matches.

Insta feed.

If you have website traffic and want to convert those people into Instagram followers, you should check out Insta feed. So, this is a Shopify app that will display your Instagram feed beautifully on your Shopify store. And it also includes a link to allow people to visit your page and follow you right away. It will increase your follower count, especially if you have a busy website already.

TikTok.

TikTok has impressive potential to reach a vast audience. By growing your TikTok account, you can convert these followers into Instagram followers as well. So start by ensuring that your Instagram account is connected to your TikTok profile. If you're interested in seeing how to grow a TikTok account as well, make sure that you're leaving me a comment down below, and if enough of you are interested, I will be more than happy to make a video on that as well. Instagram is a great tool to get people talking about your brand, but if you have a product or a service to sell, you're going to need a platform where customers can go ahead and make those purchases.

Shopify

Shopify is a great place to start. Selling online with your e-commerce website has never been easier. It's never been faster, it's never been more scalable, and setting up your store can be done in a matter of days, all by yourself. You don't need a fancy coder to do the work for you. You can get started with a free 14-day trial, no credit card required, and there's no commitment at all. These free 14 days will give you some time to build a branded personalized e-commerce store so that you can start making money on Instagram.

We could go on and on with the list of tools that can be used to promote whatever you are doing on your platforms, but with these tools also, you can create magic and begin to see a rapid improvement in your brand growth. Most of the time, app trends tend to come and go, so ensure that you remain at it, keep follow-up energy, and keep your ears to the ground to flow with the next big thing.

Chapter Three
The Tik-Tok Prospect

One way or the other, you must have come in contact with this new platform Tik-Tok, but you might be feeling a little bit skeptical. With questions like "How am I going to leverage this platform for business growth?" going through your mind. This session will give a detailed overview and feed your mind with the information it needs. The app downloads surpassed 1.5 billion in 2019, making it the second most downloaded app. Which I think is mind-blowing, and their estimates that by the end of 2020, Tik-Tok will be the number one social media app, crazy, right? We will dive into the demographics, unpack the behind-the-scenes of Tik-Tok and see how businesses can and should leverage this platform for growth. I know the fear that you may have, you may say, there's no way my audience is on Tik-Tok. Let's talk a bit about demographics and decide if this is the right platform for you and your business.

One thing that surprises most business owners to learn is that nearly 30% of Tik-Tok users are over 30. 30% of one billion is a lot. There are currently 150 different countries represented on Tik-Tok. 65% of Tik-Tok users are female. During a recent interview with Tik-Tok Corporate, they confirmed that they're working to get that balance as close to 50/50 as possible. It means that you may see a real surge of athletes in an attempt to win over the males that are still hanging out on Twitter. Tik-Tok is learning your interest, and until you have followed quite a few profiles and engaged with people, it's going to be difficult for Tik-Tok to know what to serve you. However, if you keep engaging with the content you like and skipping the content you don't, you will quickly discover that you have an entirely different experience. In recent years there's been a surge of consumers begging for a natural look at the authentic behind the scenes of brands, celebrities, and businesses. We found that consumers were falling in love with brands all over again. Instead of the perfect photo like Instagram, suddenly you're able to show the culture behind the scenes. Maybe you're super fun, perhaps you're super snarky or skeptical, that can deliver on Tik-Tok, it allows your consumers to say yep, I always knew I liked that brand, and now I understand why. Currently, quite possibly, one of the most extraordinary reasons to use Tik-Tok is that there is unlimited untapped viral potential unlike any other platform right now. Stars are being made overnight, and businesses are blowing up. For me, the first signs of potential virality were this time when a client had about 60 followers on Tik-Tok. She put up a video, and overnight, it reached 9000 views. It opened my own eyes as a content creator to the potential for virality for any business. I wanted to test it in my industry and see how it could work, so we created another video breaking down false beliefs in the marketing industry. What was so crazy was that the video went viral in a week, reaching nearly a million views and generating more YouTube subscribers than we had ever had before, the website traffic and actual sales rivaling these sales that we generate from our Facebook Ad spend every single month.

Now, originally tick-tock started with a lot of very young people like Generation Z or the Generation alpha, and some of their videos were a little bit cringe. Still, now it's growing and expanding as a platform. It's undeniable that there is a lot of marketing potential for businesses, so if you run a business and consider any social media marketing. You're ignoring tick-tock then I think you need to read this session to understand better the potential for tick-tock, how many users it has, and how you could be using Tik-Tok to make more money and a more successful marketing plan going forward in this session, I will break down essentially what Tik-Tok is, and why you might want to use it and how you should expect to use it if you decide to use tick-tock in your marketing plan.

Beginning with "what is tick-tock," it has been named the fastest growing app in 2019. It started three years ago as a musical and has 500 million users as of 2019. It's challenging to acquire a precise figure because it's spreading. According to statistics, tik-tok gained 118 million users in the first quarter of 2019, resulting in a massive shortage of creators. People who start creating on tick-tock draw so much faster than they would on Instagram, Facebook, Twitter, or any other platform that is beginning to get a little more saturated, implying that tick-tock has a lot of growth potential and a large user base. We will get into what kind of businesses should be considering tick-tock. People spend more and more time on this app; it's totally and ravishingly spreading among the younger people and starting to move up. Now, as you'll be getting into using this app, I will make a detailed explanation of how to set it up, but before that, the billion-dollar question is, "what businesses should really be considering tick-tock when you're looking at your marketing plan."

The first and most apparent group would be the influencers or marketers. That is talking about people that are basically just out there, who are just popular based on the kind of content they have been delivering over time, and are making money from sponsored posts, where they're advertising for like makeup, or they're advertising for a watch. Now, because they have grown a considerable influence already, people follow them, and because they have an extensive network, companies will come and say, hey, if you wear our watch, we'll give you, you know, $5,000 or more. Now, just because of the influence they have on a large number of people, they will definitely be great for tick-tock, and that is because they can proliferate, and their audience is all that matters; the size of the audience. It's not so much about the click-through rate and other factors like that for them because over time, it's been realized that one of the significant drawbacks with Tik-Tok right now is it's a little bit tricky to monetize, as you don't have the likes of links and URLs like you have on YouTube. You don't get paid for ads like you would on YouTube. Tic-Tok ads are obviously a compelling way, and it's such a large platform right now you can definitely get a lot of exposure, and the ads are something that you should definitely be considering.

The Four Es

Now, there are four E's that I look at every time I am talking or writing about diving into Tik-Tok marketing strategy, and these Es will be discussed below, but before we do that, I'd like to first deal with some things. Now, if you're still feeling skeptical, head on over to the Tik-Tok app right now and go type in the hashtag for your industry, maybe it's hashtag plumbing, perhaps it's hashtag lead generation, perhaps it's hashtag entrepreneurs or hashtag life insurance and checks it out because if your hashtag is there, there's viability for your business on Tik-Tok. The beautiful thing with Tik-Tok is that it is a closed ecosystem; you can link your profile to your YouTube, drive people to your website, drive them to lead magnets. Another opportunity that is just emerging is *"Tik-Tok Ads."* Let me bring something to your attention. I've had a sneak peek behind the scenes, and the CPMs are juicy, the reach is incredible, and the targeting is improving every day. Now, I plan to answer some of the questions about Tik-Tok: What is the point of being on Tik-Tok?. Let us now proceed to discuss these Es;

Education

Entertainment

Engagement

Emotion

If you can tap into these four Es, you will have your loyal customers saying yes and your new markets and audience reached on Tik-Tok saying yes.

Education

The first step with education is to educate your consumers on this platform. For example, I've seen some videos that say, here is what an adequately laid floor looks like, and they show examples of an excellent base versus the shoddy work from one of their competitors. It's beautiful, and businesses can educate their consumers on what they should be looking for, and in fact, that leaves consumers feeling incredibly empowered and trusting you as the right solution for whatever they need to buy.

Entertainment

Secondly, talk about entertainment. The truth is we all like to be entertained, right? Doesn't matter how introverted you are; something must catch your interest, irrespective of how fun or how non-fun it might seem; you want entertainment one way or the other. Some go to movies, perhaps even Netflix binge each evening, listen there's no shame, but your customers are the same way, who doesn't love watching a great series or a movie that keeps them on the edge of their seat? Tik-Tok is no different; in fact, the average Tik-Tok user is spending 61 minutes per day on the app, and 75% of that time is spent on the For You page searching for new content, new profiles to follow, and that could be your businesses content that they're binging in tonight.

Engagement

Thirdly, Engagement. Everybody loves to find people who are similar to them, so when people are scrolling on Tik-Tok, and they find content that makes them say oh, I thought I was the only one, they're so excited to engage because suddenly you've given them permission to say, I feel the same way, or I'm eager to learn about this. You can create literal engagement bait on Tik-Tok, and audiences are eating it up.

Emotions

Now for the fourth E, and this is, in my opinion, the most powerful is Emotion. When you can start to tap into stories, maybe it's the stories of some of your customers whose lives have been changed by your products, perhaps it's a before-and-after that leaves someone feeling incredibly inspired, maybe it was that mission that your team took to another country to impact the world, and you're able to tell the story making people feel good, making them feel happy, making them feel hopeful. When you can touch on Emotion on Tik-Tok, you'll be amazed to see how audiences spring to life. People love to cry, laugh, laugh, and love to, even as crazy as it sounds, get angry, especially when something goes against their values, and this is the perfect place to connect with them emotionally.

The Tic-Tok prospect

Now there are certain types of businesses that are most prime for Tik-Tok, and those are anything that is B2C, especially E-commerce, physical products, apparel, anything you're selling directly to a consumer is excellent for Tik-Tok, anything that has a beautiful aesthetic. Beauty, food blogging, luxury real estate ready for the Tik-Tok market, and any business that naturally has a hero or a spokesperson for the brand make a lot of sense for them to be on Tik-Tok. Now, as promised, I'm going to blow your mind with several examples of big businesses and small businesses that are absolutely crushing it on Tik-Tok.

First up, we have Chipotle, which launched a campaign on Tik-Tok all about avocados. It

Increased their Guac sales for the following week after their campaign by over 63%.

Next up, we have Calvin Klein. Calvin Klein launched a massive traditional media campaign featuring Justin Bieber in Calvin Klein underwear. When they launched their very first Tik-Tok campaign within 24 hours, they surpassed the total number of engagements of that entire traditional media campaign with just their Tik-Tok meetings alone.

We've all heard the song, Old Town Road by Lil Nas X, ♪ I'm gonna take my horse to the old town road, ♪ ♪ I'm gonna ride till I can't no more. ♪ That song hit peak popularity 100% thanks to Tik-Tok. Before that song's release, Lil Nas X was unheard of in the music industry, and through marketing on Tik-Tok, that song became the number one most streamed single of all time. But let's take it a little more practical because that's a really extreme example of what Tik-Tok marketing can do.

Next up, The Bentist is the famous dentist from West rock Ortho, who grew from one location to three with just Tik-Tok marketing alone. Now there's a hidden gem in Tik-Tok, and that is sponsorships. Many of the influencers on Tik-Tok have never been influencers before, and there's not a going rate for support. In fact, just the other day, I spoke to an influencer who is a famous blogger; she had 160,000 followers on Tik-Tok with millions of views. And I asked her what her going rate was for a sponsored post, and she said $25 per sponsored post. So the ability to partner with influencers in a way that's A, more easily tracked, B, more cost-effective, and C, ultimately potentially able to even go viral, is honestly unmatched by any other platform.

Now Let's begin to discuss how you as a product provider can start to harness the power of the Tok, how you can play in the but league games, talking about how you can find and secure sponsorships with influencers even if you're not on the Tik-Tok platform yourself or as a business.

Step one: You're going to search for a hashtag that your ideal audience might use, and you will find the influencers that are putting out top content within that hashtag. Now here's the beautiful thing, you can go straight to their profile, click through to their Instagram and send them a message on Instagram asking them for their rates. The beautiful thing is, you're gonna find, you may just have better results reach, engagement, and ultimately sales than you ever did on any other platform. Understanding how you can monetize Tik-Tok through sponsorships and finding your dream influencers. These are what you'd be sifting through as we proceed. Now one of the best ways to decide if Tik-Tok is a good investment for you and your business is to spend some time on the app, give it a go, test it out, shoot some videos.

Chapter Four
The Pinterest Prospect

Here we will comprehensively discuss an effective Pinterest marketing strategy for your business. The idea here is to help you as a business owner or a blogger to use Pinterest to grow your business and revenue online. Now we will go over this 10-step system of coming up with a simple yet effective Pinterest marketing strategy that will help you grow on Pinterest and boost the traffic and revenue in your online business.

Now, if you're a business or a blogger, you can use Pinterest like any other social media or search engine to grow your business, and the best way to do this is by setting a clear plan of how you want to use Pinterest strategically, so you never invest your precious time into strategies that don't work or take too much time. First, let us familiarize ourselves with this platform's whole concept. What Pinterest marketing is, why it is essential for your online business.

Pinterest is a social media platform where you can share images you create or find online with other pinners, these images and other visuals are then searchable on the platform which makes it a substantial visual search engine similar like google but just with these images here so if I had to come up with a definition, I would say that Pinterest marketing is how you strategically use Pinterest to grow the traffic to your website and blog and this includes creating your own content, say blog content or products and then create dedicated pinnable images to be pinned so you can share on Pinterest for each of those pieces of content and Pinterest users can then search for these pins and click on them and are led back to your website which grows your traffic so Pinterest marketing includes everything from how you come up with a Pinterest content strategy, how you optimize and grow your account and profile to Pinterest SEO to how to use Pinterest to increase the traffic and revenue in your online business. Now the million-dollar question is, "why is Pinterest marketing important in the first place." Getting people to your website and blog is essential; you want to get as many eyes on your content as possible to build an audience, get comments and replies and maybe make some money with ads or sponsored content. When you're a business, it is essential to get new clients and precisely the right people to your site to make an income, right? And there are many ways to grow traffic online, but talking about Pinterest, this tool in itself has become one of the favorites amongst bloggers. It's so effective that businesses start to jump on as well, and you can now not only promote your website but also your product if you are, for example, an online shop, google, and other strategies can take a long time to see results, but on Pinterest, you can see results fast, and that's why people love it so much Pinterest is easier and faster than other strategies.

The Pinterest Prospect

Now you need to be super clear on why you're on Pinterest, so we're talking about your goals and whom you want to attract. There are over 450 million monthly users on Pinterest right now not every one of these people is going to be a good fit for your brand, so I want you to write down who your ideal customer avatar is your so-called ICA (Ideal Client Avatar) who is your dream reader or customer what age and gender is this person what is this person into? What do they struggle with? Then think about how your blog or business is going to help them. Is your content going to inspire, relate, educate or simply bring some fun into this person's life? How can your products solve this person's problem and make their lives happier or more relaxed?

This exercise will assist you in creating content that attracts the right people to the Pinterest app; you don't want to speak to everyone once you're clear on that, you'll have a super easy time coming up with blog post ideas and product ideas, and you'll also know more about which language you should speak to on your pins or in your pin descriptions to address those people so that you attract the right kind of people from Pinterest to your brand, business, or blog now that you're clear on that

I recommend you start with a new Pinterest business account. A Pinterest business account is free, but it unlocks all kinds of cool features like analytics or claiming your website; you don't want to use your account for your blog or business first of all if you're using Pinterest for business or making money through Pinterest, Pinterest states in their terms of views that you need a business account

Create your Pinterest boards. Your Pinterest boards contain all your pins. You save or pin to your account so you can create a pin, and then you upload it to Pinterest, but before it becomes public to Pinterest users, you need to save it to one of your boards, so boards are like folders on your computer and pins are like the documents you store in them. So, boards are a way of organizing your profile. Now, if you're a business selling ice cream, for example, you could create boards around ice cream flavors or homemade ice cream tutorials; if you're a travel blogger, you could make boards around destinations like countries, for example, Italy, Spain, France, or you could create boards around travel interests say hiking snorkeling paragliding or just hanging at the pool and relaxing.

Come up with your content strategy and plan now; if you're a blogger, you got this covered, but if you're a business, I want you to think about how you can come up with regular weekly content to share on your Pinterest profile. Pinterest wants you to share new inspiring content which will help you attract your audience; this means creating weekly content around your business so yes, start a blog where you share either regular blog posts or your podcast episodes or content from your social media like your videos. Your blog then becomes this place where you regularly share relevant new content in addition to the products you sell that you can share to your Pinterest account; this way, each week, you'll have something new to share with your audience on Pinterest, and you're constantly creating new opportunities for people to find you on Pinterest now yes this is additional work, but it's worth it in the long run.

Create your pins. Pins are images you specifically create for Pinterest that you post to the platform and then lead back to your account. Your pins are how people can find your fantastic profile and products, so this is an essential step. You can create many different pin types; there are regular pen images and video pins, recipe pins, and product pins now; this is where your product and blog contents come in. You are to start creating pins for your existing blog posts every time you make a new piece of content. You should also create pins for your product now. If you are an online shop, you can use free design tools like canvas or tailwind create to input a title, a description, and an image, and the device will come up with hundreds of pen designs in literally minutes. Now, once you've designed your pens, you're going to save them to your board so they become public, and Pinterest distributes them to the Pinterest users. By now, you are already halfway through your Pinterest marketing strategy.

You are learning about Pinterest SEO. Now, SEO stands for Search Engine Optimization. It sounds super complicated, but that is precisely why you are reading this right now: to have a breakdown of every social media jargon you will ever encounter. Currently, there are thousands of pins saved to Pinterest every day, and Pinterest has billions of pins already reserved, so how does Pinterest know which pin is relevant for someone when they are searching. For example, wedding inspiration on Pinterest; is where the Pinterest algorithm comes in. The Pinterest algorithm looks at your profile. It looks at your boards, it seems at your pins and your website, and then analyzes everything to understand what you are all about, then it shows your pins to people who might be interested. Now, you can use Pinterest SEO to optimize your account and pins to help the Pinterest algorithm understand your business or blog even better, and this will help your pins reach more and more people and show up higher in the Pinterest search when someone types in a keyword. I want to enlighten you about how Pinterest SEO works in this SEO strategy. Now, the basics are that you know how to optimize your account, and what's important to consider when you pin to Pinterest is that you see massive success fast.

Use tools and services to automate. On Pinterest, consistency is super important, basically like every other social media, and you want to show up with new content regularly, so you become the go-to person for that topic for your audience. Now, there's so much on Pinterest that you can automate. Automation is excellent on Pinterest, and you can use these tools, and you're still going to see a ton of success. There is a scheduler called tailwind which is used to automate your pinning process on Pinterest fully; all you have to do is upload your pins to tailwind and then set a schedule, and then tailwind automatically posts your pins to Pinterest at the perfect time for your audience while you lay asleep.

Grow your email list. It's essential that you also grow an audience off of Pinterest; yes, your Pinterest followers matter and they are great, but it's like with every social account, it does not belong to you. Sometimes I hear about people whose Pinterest accounts got banned or shut down for legit reasons or not; you don't own your Pinterest account, so you must grow your audience off the platform where you've got the control. So, growing an email list is so important, and an email list is when you set up an account with convert-kit as a separate service. Then you start collecting emails from people who visit your blog or shop over from Pinterest once they're on your email list, you have control over when you send out an email about a new blog post or item in your shop, and then a third business email is also one of the most effective ways on how to make money online. Imagine having a thousand email subscribers, and you just created a brand-new product; this means you can send them an email letting them know about your new offer. Your email will land in their inbox as no third party like Pinterest or an algorithm between you and your audience. An email list is a must for every blogger and business owner, and I recommend you start one as soon as you can if you haven't.

As I get towards dropping my pen, another point to note is the need to develop your online money-making plan. You've built a fantastic website or blog, and your Pinterest account is doing great, bringing all these amazing new people over to your space but now what? How will this make you more money or turn that blog of yours into an actual side hustle or even a full-time income?

There are so many ways how you can make money online. You can sell your products or services, use affiliate marketing to make money with ads, or get brands to sponsor your content. You need to sit and figure out what makes the most sense for your business.

It is also essential to understand that just because you have this account on Pinterest and people click on your website link does not mean you are making money online. If you want to make money online, you still need a business, and you still need to sell something, a product or your service, you need to make offers, you need to be paid for ads running on your site. You want to become crystal clear on what you're selling in your online business and how you're planning on making money. If that's your goal, write it down and become very clear on how you're going to achieve your goal. From here, I want you to analyze and repeat what works for you. Now, you also need to understand that data is so powerful, and once you get into a rhythm of pinning on Pinterest, you'll learn what resonates with your audience and what falls flat, you will see trends and be able to create more and more of what's working, and this right here is how you're going to grow your account fast. Repeat what's repeatedly working; it will build trust with Pinterest and your audience and learn to see what your pinners are struggling with the most and how your blogger products can help them. The longer you analyze and repeat what's working, the better you're going to get at Pinterest marketing; you're going to gain confidence in your Pinterest, and it's going to become second nature. Go into your analytics, develop some benchmarks and numbers you plan to track each month to see your progress in black and white, and then keep working and refining your Pinterest marketing strategy, so you get better and better at it.

Chapter Five
Facebook Marketing

Talking about Facebook marketing, this platform alone has helped people get massive results. Writing about leveraging on Facebook marketing in this time couldn't be more educative or fun. Product providers have been able to reach millions of people, generate millions of websites clicks, and produce millions of sales, all while strictly using Facebook marketing

This session will go over everything you need to know about generating tangible results using Facebook. Now obviously, there are many marketing channels to choose from, you have traditional marketing that plays like magazines, billboards, and cold calling, and then you have digital marketing that plays like blogging, google, and social media, so why Facebook? On the surface, it just looks like a place where people connect with their friends, right, so does it offer any real business value? The truth is, Facebook has two essential elements that allow them to stand out from every other marketing channel in the world and the first one is that they have

A user base of over one billion users and you can reach almost anyone who's in your target market on Facebook.

The ability to hold attention. The average U.S adult spends 38 minutes per day consuming Facebook content, and for context, users spend an average of five seconds looking at a website's written content, and that 38 minutes was just on Facebook that doesn't even account for all their other digital platforms like Instagram.

Facebook Marketing

Now, this session is broken into three parts in the first part. We are going to look at Facebook from the organic side, which is all the free features available to businesses like you in the second part, we are going to look at Facebook from the pay side, which looks at all their paid ad features, and in the third part, we are going to look at the combinations and predictions for Facebook going forward.

Facebook organic marketing

Now, the first thing you need to know is that there's a personal side of Facebook and there's a business side of Facebook the majority of these users only use the private side so that's the typical stuff like creating posts sharing content and talking with friends but there's an entirely different side of Facebook which is the business side so if you own a business or working for a company and you are ready to get started then the first thing you need to do is set up a business manager by going to *business.facebook.com* and create an account from here you can start building your Facebook business assets like your Facebook page, your ad account your catalog pixels and more the main thing that you need to know for organic Facebook marketing is your Facebook page in fact nearly everything you do on Facebook business wise will relate back to your page, because your Facebook page is like your hub it's kind of like your personal website but on Facebook's platform so it's really important that you set your page up for success and you know all the features available to you so let's take a few minutes to look at your Facebook page. Now let us discuss some on-screen features that Facebook offers you as a user.

Facebook organic marketing is free marketing, and who doesn't love free? For example, our YouTube channel as a content creating brand is a part of our organic strategy, and we've gone into this year with the expectation that it's going to take a while before it takes off, which means, in the beginning, you will likely see a slow rise in traffic fans or sales so taking the organic route means you're willing to put in the effort and the time.

Now let us discuss four organic tips starting with tip number one;

Create valuable content. The critical takeaway is to give your audience value and avoid selling. It doesn't matter how great your page looks or how many features your page uses if the content is terrible, remember Facebook is a place where people genuinely go to connect with other people, so if you are interrupting that, you better be bringing in some massive value.

Create valuable native content. Native content is simply content that purely lives on the platform. That is important because Facebook has a complex algorithm that helps determine what content they should show to its users, and we found that Facebook posts with links to other places like blogs will get far less reach. There's a time and a place to promote your site, but remember Facebook's goal is to keep their user's attention, so they don't want you and millions of other companies spamming their users with links because if so, then people will stop using Facebook and that's not what you want, and neither does Facebook which is why you want to create valuable content that makes people want to consume share and discuss with. Speaking of discussions, if you're able to spark a positive debate, that can be a quick hack to get more engagement and more reach; however, I would recommend staying away from political or social issues because that can put you in a compromising position.

Use video content. Facebook's goal is to increase their user's attention their time on the platform, so they've already nailed down native range, and now they're focusing more on video engagement, so if you're creating video content right now, you're going to get a significant boost in the algorithm that means more people will share your content and remember the video needs to be all about your audience and bringing them value now hopefully this can help you create a winning content plan

Community development. If you already have traffic and many fans and you need to promote your Facebook page to them, but if you're starting from scratch, then my biggest recommendation would be to start or join Facebook groups because the Facebook algorithm is significantly diminished in a Facebook group setting so that you can reach many people. When you enter a Facebook group, there are usually some moderation rules which in general, most group owners don't want you to spam their members with your sales or your links, so can you guess the most effective way to leverage a group if you said to provide valuable content then you think right when you give good advice feedback or content in a group setting then people naturally want to learn more about you, and you can position your Facebook group or your Facebook page in a way where people can find those assets and become fans, so that takes care of part one of the sessions which is organic marketing

Facebook Paid Ads

The paid side of Facebook marketing is often referred to as Facebook advertising products, which allows you to grow your content and your audience much faster. The first thing you need to know about Facebook advertising is a Facebook ad account. You can set up a Facebook ad account by logging into your business manager and simply creating an ad account, and again, you can go to business.facebook.com to get started. Now, let's say we want to go after some dog lovers. Here we have the objective, and we want to send traffic to the website. You can select a daily budget or even a lifetime budget, and then you can also pick a start date and an end date which is all optional, then you have the audience. You can choose your specific location and target a particular age group or age range. You can choose from different demographics different interests and behaviors that people put out on Facebook.

Some demographics of dog lovers could be groups and people who are dog lovers, and that would be an interest. You can also go after a demographic such as dog groomers, dog trainers, dog walkers, and dog handlers. Once you can make these demographic specifications, you will start getting suggestions of people who are interested in puppies, people who are dog walkers, people who are just interested in dogs or dog health or dog training, people who have pets at home, people interested in dog behavior pet groomers pet stores. You will be given so many options to choose from, and then you can layer these options by narrowing the audience. If we say we want to target these two interests and want them to match another interest, you have to understand the concept of behavioral strategy. Now, let's just say you know this person is an engaged shopper, and maybe this person also has an anniversary coming up within the next 61 to 90 days. Now, there are so many different options and leverage to pull here, but the point is that it is a very sophisticated targeting system and very powerful, and I highly doubt if you would not find your audience using this system.

You have probably seen ads before, but to ensure that you have every information you will need, you need to know that there are a lot of different formats you can choose from; single images or video images, carousel ads collection ads you can even do slide shows and more. This is where you start communicating the value you give to your audience. By now, looking keenly, you can begin to see some of the power within the Facebook ads manager. Statistics have repeatedly shown that the Facebook ads manager is a compelling platform, but let's remember that it is a pay-to-play platform, and its primary value prompt is giving you the ability to reach people faster, but you have to be willing to pay enough. Now let us further discuss some more tips.

Think with the end in mind; this is from one of my favorite quotes from *Stephen covey,* which reigns true even within Facebook marketing and other warriors you want to know your desired outcome before you start advertising. Is it reach, is it engagement, is it traffic, is its app to be installed? Now, most of our clients are looking for leads or sales, but if you don't have a compulsive deal or a warm audience, you may need to start by building up a fan base. Most people won't buy from you during the first interaction; according to HubSpot, the average number of touchpoints needed to get to a sale is eight, so you may need a combination of posts, emails, website visits, or phone calls before a prospect buys from you and someone who has already started this journey will be considered a part of your warm audience.

Start small: If you're just starting or you have not quite figured out Facebook advertising yet, then you don't need to go out and blow 10 000 a month; instead, I would recommend starting with a modest budget of about 1000 to 1500 per month which should give you enough data quickly to fine-tune your audience, and creative secondly don't start by pitching your most expensive offer instead offer something small you can offer something free like a free guide or exclusive video in exchange for an email address or something smaller. Start with low offers to get the ball rolling and establish some trust. My advice is to take a slow and steady approach when building a new relationship. The only exception to this is if you have an impulsive buy; for example, if you're selling some delicious cookies and as soon as someone sees it, they're tempted to buy, and you definitely should start with your fixed price.

Track everything; The most significant advantage of Facebook and other digital marketing platforms is their ability to measure your results with precision. You can see everything from impressions to the same dollar return that you got on your ads. This means you want to make sure you're installing Facebook pixels on your website that way, you can cookie the visitors that go to your website from Facebook. Then you can track exactly how your visitors engage from Facebook to your website now if you're selling a product on Facebook shopping feature, then this is native, and you can track sales from within Facebook ads manager on your Facebook shopping store of which you need to remember that the more native you can be the better effect that it can have on the algorithm.

Those are my top three tips when it comes to Facebook advertising. Now let's wrap up with the final part three of this session here. We will look at how to keep winning using the above combinations and then make speculations for Facebook marketing moving forward from here. We have established that the best outcome for

Facebook marketing is to use both organic and ads advertising methods. Now, let's take a look at a marketing funnel. We will be using an example of a personal trainer. Now, depending on the product you're selling (personal training), you'll need to provide some great exercise plans and advice as part of your organic approach. The following section is your engagement section; where we want to grow our fans and engagement as much as possible, so we're going to start boosting some of those posts, which is now a part of your paid strategy; these first two phrases go hand in hand because you want to build a sizable audience, so let's say we're going after maybe 25 000 fans now once you get to about 25 000 fans you're ready to start making an offer and since you're. All your lovers have to do is give you their name, their email address, their number and book a time to sign up, and so now you're in the consideration phase of the marketing funnel, and you have their email their number, and you're ready to start selling. That will be your warm audience now that you're ready to start emailing, texting, and calling your prospects to talk about buying your core product, which may be your monthly training services. We've combined organic and paid strategies and completed an entire marketing funnel in this example. Now there are endless ways to incorporate organic and paid strategies; for example, you could create an event, advertise it and then follow it up with social media posts, so the key here is to attempt to meet your customers where they are.

Now, let's go ahead and round off this session with the last thing on my mind: Facebook marketing moving forward and beyond. As you can tell with this material guide, Facebook is a company that is still very aggressive in its platform's growth. Facebook favors brands that favor their users. It's a win-win for everybody, so what are some things that Facebook as a marketing platform is pushing right. As I highlighted earlier, videos are becoming more and more critical, as it helps Facebook increase the time spent on their platform, and I believe that long-form video will have a significant advantage in the algorithm as we advance into coming years. Also, I think you're going to see an explosion of growth with Facebook shops because it keeps users on their platform, and it's native, so don't wait. Go ahead and start using some of these content features and producing long-form videos.

Conclusion

After going over everything that has been said, we can come to a conclusion by summarizing everything into these;

Online presence on social media networks is increasing; social media is becoming more popular. Facebook, Twitter, LinkedIn, and Instagram are all growing in popularity. They are now an excellent way to expand your business's growth. Other social media networks, such as Pinterest, Instagram, and Snapchat, are gaining traction in photo and video content and attracting a more comprehensive range of demographics.

Produce content for each social media platform; Create content for your chosen media network. You cannot post the same content on multiple networks simultaneously. So, when it comes to content writing, be inventive.

Social media is a digital marketing tool for telling stories rather than selling products. You can use it to sell your products directly. However, it is more effective to tell them stories about your products to be more engaged with your content.

More graphic, photo, and video content; Make more graphic images, videos, and photos to engage your customers. When displaying your products in it, the quality should be excellent. To create and share more of this type of content.

Conduct promotional and contest activities; You should hold more contests and promotional activities to gain the attention and participation of your target market. Using various digital tools, you can make these activity announcements more effective.

Contents based on research; The content of your post or image should be based on research. You should understand what you're writing about. When displaying facts and figures or quoting existing information, use accurate facts and figures.

More emphasis on mobile social media; 70% of smartphone users use mobile social apps. As a result, you should concentrate your efforts on mobile social media apps. It is an effective method for gaining more users.

Quick response to comments, complaints, and feedback; social media is now handled by the social media department in many companies. People can inquire about you at any time, and they expect you to respond quickly to their questions, complaints, feedback, and comments. As a result, always respond to them as soon as possible. It will increase your work efficiency.

In today's world, the possibilities for using social media are nearly limitless, and the only limitation is your own imagination. To summarize, you will agree with me that we are in a better position now than we were ten years ago in terms of marketing and placing items in the broader viewing range. The Internet has already changed people's lives, and social media has added to that optimism by making selling and buying faster and more efficient, thus making the jobs of product providers and sellers easier. This will work for those willing to put in the time and effort, and it will be a massive money-making operation.

SOCIAL MEDIA MARKETING FOR BEGINNERS 2023

Learn how to grow your social media with beginner's strategy updated for this specific year; this book provides you easy and organized knowledge ready for you

TOM RUELL

Introduction

Let us quickly go back in time, say 2002, and suppose you want to make a document public or a book and also set up a blog; you are probably sure that you'd be successful, but you are only worried about one thing, you do not know how to make sure that this book of yours reaches the intended recipient audience, or who could enjoy this book. However, just a few types of advertising were available during that time, such as print ads, billboards, radio, direct mail, direct sales, and television. All of these methods were prohibitively expensive, whose efficacy could not be determined, and which did not allow you to advertise your content to a proper audience, implying that your book would never reach the audience it deserved. Now let us look into and pay attention to this very same scenario in the present day, alongside traditional forms of advertising. You would have entree to digital marketing as a method of marketing that's a lot more profitable and price-reasonable and configurable marketing that would aid marketers to advertise to their listeners digitally using mediums like search engines, websites, social media platforms, emails, to mention a few. Among these types, social media marketing seems like the most eye-catching. Social media marketing would give you as a product deliverer the prospect to take advantage of social media platforms to publicize your content to a highly targeted audience. It would also help more people learn about your book and increase the interaction with your audience, and the best part is that it is relatively inexpensive unless you go into advertising. This whole social media platform will also help you get marketplace insights that might help in understanding your audience preferences better. Let us further assume that you started by taking up a certification process to learn about social media marketing. Since you are already familiar with the whole concept of social media marketing, your next step will be to learn about the different types of content you could display on social media. Some of the most public forms of content you could post would be images, text, posts, polls, and videos. Still, over time you will probably begin to notice that not many people are being exposed to your content anymore.

You start to realize that you need to advertise your content for specific channels, that you would have to employ the advertising alternatives offered by social media networks such as Facebook, Instagram, YouTube, Linked-in, and Twitter as most of these advertising platforms offer users several different options such as image ads. These ads comprise solo or numerous descriptions that are nice-looking and have the optimum quantity of writing. They also include a rallying cry that stimulates user participation. You can now use images from your book to advertise on websites that sell your book and more. Currently, there are texts and post ads. These ads could promote posts or excerpts from your blog or your book, further garnering interest from an exciting audience.

You might also employ video advertisements that include favourable reviews and customer testimonials to advertise to your readers, and you could also use lead ads through which you could collect information from users involved in a weekly newsletter or regular updates from your blog. But the truth is that these are not the only things you could do with social media channels; you could create a brand for yourself and drive audience interest, engage with them, create an identity, engage with content, and find content that works for them you. Social media platforms will also allow you to develop audiences based on demographics such as their age, location, gender, and much more, and over time you will see an increase in the number of visitors coming to your social media page, and therefore your blog. You will also see an increase in the total number of individuals who bought your book, significantly increasing your audience. This book has some of the most crucial things to learn about social media marketing, a step-by-step approach for getting your goods out there and getting massive returns and pulling in relevant attention, and a moderate upturn in profit and presence creation of your brand and product.

Some of the things addressed in this book include;

How to set quantitative, intelligent goals and follow a constant deadline.

How to understand your audience by engaging and connecting with them

How to set up a social media calendar to plan competitions polls, surveys, videos, and more

How to use tools for lead generation creating email lists, setting buyer personas, and more

How to perform visual storytelling with the help of images and videos

Now the question that might be bothering you could be that how would I be able to lay my hands on all of these?

Before we begin to shed more light on these questions, let's ask ourselves these questions. What can you do with social media marketing? How does engaging with your audience play a vital role in marketing? What is the relevance of your method of determining your target market based on demographics?

All these questions will answer your questions when we begin to answer them.

Chapter One
Startup

You would agree with me if I said the world that we live in now is a highly digital place, but the reality is; that wasn't always the case until four years ago, so if we rewind, letting people know about your products was a little more complicated then, so even if you go back say five or ten years in time, promoting your products wasn't as easy as it is today. People had to resort to good old-fashioned newspapers, putting an ad on those big thick books called the Yellow Pages that usually sat in your closet and weighed a ton. These and more were ways through which people had to get their product and service out there even though it seems so archaic looking at it now, but back then, that was legitimate, that was the way to do it, and then suddenly, one thing made our lives a lot easier. It came and disrupted the space of marketing. Now let us begin to answer some of these questions keeping us at the edge of our chairs since we picked up this book. I will tag this part as "Introduction to the edge." You know how you can have the edge over a whole lot of other people just because you have a piece of information that they do not have or you are aware of something that they have no idea. We will begin to pay attention to this part of the story here.

How to have "the edge" over others

How can you get started with social media marketing so you can stand out from the crowd by utilizing this fantastic platform that we all use today? First, let us define the core notion, which is what social media marketing is in and of itself: social media marketing.

"Social media marketing involves increasing website traffic it centres engagement it offers you the ability to increase your brand awareness, and it has other marketing goals so you can create various forms of content for different social media platforms."

So that's really in a nutshell what social media marketing in itself is. That is basic, generally known information. The quest is usually to increase our traffic or engagement like the likes or comments; you need to understand marketing principles on social media platforms. Engaging with our users, customers, and potential and prospective clients can put a personalized experience using social media marketing. If the idea is to create different forms of content like videos and blogs and infographics and other types of graphics with the potential actually to go viral and what we would mean viral is spreading like wildfire, one user sending it to another as rapidly as can be and before you know it you get millions of views and millions of likes. That right there is social media's influence on marketing. The following question would be the "WHY" why we need to do social media marketing? We have probably partially responded to this question in the last part, but let's dig a little deeper. We mentioned in our definition of marketing on social media that are we have the opportunity to build our brand awareness, and that is no more truthful than with social media marketing, more so than any other digital marketing channel. We can improve our brand by pushing out appropriate content to reasonable people using social media marketing. It allows us to put our brand in a good light, in a good position in the vicinity of the right eyeballs, allowing us to put our brand in a good place in front of the right eyeballs, allowing us to improve our brand by pushing out appropriate content in front of reasonable people. For this, social media is a beautiful platform. We can also look at conversion rates to see if we're presenting the right product or service in front of the right individuals.

We build a funnel of prospective customers who turn loyal customers into lifetime customers. We could see it, at every step in the process, that our conversion rates may increase, we can undoubtedly leverage social media marketing for SEO (Search Engine Optimization) for search engine rankings, which is basically about posting content on social media platforms to build up the most efficient traffic. We need to understand that you will accede to some benefits from an efficiently working SEO and social media side-by-side; it is very cost-effective if these are efficiently and strategically combined. Now, if you're posting content on Twitter or Facebook, it doesn't cost you anything; it just might require a small amount of time and creativity. Now, if you decide to go ahead and do some advertising on these platforms, yes, it is going to cost you, but you would be surprised that it is not going to be as costly as other search platforms like saying Google or Bing, where you are paying for keywords and also paying per click for those keywords. So, social media marketing can be very cost effective and then also increase top funnel traffic, so here we begin to see that it goes all the way back to brand experience and brand awareness, as you're putting yourself in position to get noticed by your target audience and Then your target customer progresses from seeing your brand for the first time to learning more about it, the further to maybe buying a product or service from your brand and then returning to buy another product and service and then continuing to buy that product or service, this is without argument increasing the top funnel traffic, and this is not just the traffic but the conversions also, this in the long run means that at every step in the process social media allows you to build that funnel depending on where somebody is whether they're seeing your brand for the first time or actually returning to purchase the product or service again, and this right here, is the inherent benefit of these platforms, these unlimited possibilities with product consumers and clients are the intrinsic benefits of social media marketing. As we talk about social media marketing, we will most definitely need to discuss using the potential channels used for social media marketing. Social media marketing is already a channel in itself, so let's look at the platform you can use to establish social media marketing efficiently. Now, there are some prevalent platforms, so if you can't tell just by these logos, you probably have not used social media marketing or social media platforms before or taken part in social media.

The Social Media Language

These are the most popular platforms, but hundreds of social media platforms exist. When we talk about social media marketing and competing, we will begin to see anything from microblogging to video-sharing like YouTube, networking platforms like LinkedIn or say bookmarking sites or content sharing sites like Reddit, Q&A sites like Quora platforms for social media come in a variety of forms. Now let us start to address some of the most popular social media platforms, and that's Facebook.

Facebook has an average of (2.27 billion) two-point two seven billion monthly active users. That number is fluctuating since we talk about billions of monthly active users. Up to 88% of all users are on mobile, so what does that tell you? That means you that Facebook has an app and that app is viral; people tend to use the app more than they use the webpage for Facebook, as they do not necessarily need to log on via the internet on their laptops or PC; they go right to the app it's just easier to disseminate information, more accessible to add, friends, comment, respond and so on, it is then no surprise that 88% of all users use mobile now (66%) sixty-six percent of monthly mobile users use Facebook daily, so a lot of recurring users are going back on a day-to-day basis are two-thirds of the whole figure, so it's an addiction, and what Facebook offers is the opportunity to get information from the people you trust, care about and like to work with, you could also share a group with people you have a common interest with, you could also partake in the same organization, maybe have the same scheme, having the same group with the same passion, and that right there is what Facebook is, the commonality it establishes amongst people, and if you build up a network of that commonality, it is going to be addicting to take part in them. Facebook also bridges that gap between distance and sometimes the feeling of knowing that you are part of somebody's life daily by just being on Facebook is also part of what makes it addictive. Thinking further about it from an end user's perspective makes total sense. Now, if you wear your digital marketing thinking hat, you will be seeing this in the light of "Hey, two-thirds of a group of individuals or multiple users utilize it regularly, and there are billions of active users there."

Facebook is evenly matched or say distributed between males and females, so if you are having your target focused towards the older or you are skewing, the younger ones as your target audience, with half as female and half as male, then you know somewhere in there, that whomever you are targeting is going to be on Facebook just based on these numbers here. Your demographic is likely also going to be on Facebook. Now Facebook allows for video content to post videos all day long, so if you have YouTube videos, you can share those videos on Facebook; videos, just like on most platforms, tend to provide better engagement in the capitalized industries.

Now some of the most liked pages on Facebook spans across many brands but let's take a look at Coca-Cola, for example, and Coca-Cola just pretty much pinpoints everything great about what you could do on Facebook, the brand is not necessarily just pushing out only their product per se they are trying to use Facebook to build up brand awareness, so a vast fortune company like Coca-Cola is not necessarily just using Facebook to push e-commerce or to push a product, the brand is out there making what it is doing for the community this is expressly an excellent example if you can relate the leverage in this simple concept, knowing how you can leverage on what you want to portray of your brand per time and what Facebook has to offer, and that would also entail brand awareness, community building, sharing your content, updated information not only about the company as you can see in this case of Coca-Cola which is situated in Atlanta Georgia in the United States you can see what they are doing with their contents and their page, contents that relate the society and community to the brand. Now, this is a good example, and of course, it is a great example, and this is because the Coca-Cola company in itself is big and known worldwide. Still, the great thing about Facebook is you can always take a peek at what other companies are doing whether you have a million-plus people liking your page or a hundred plus people like in your page, you can always get ideas as to how they are leveraging Facebook. Now owning a brand or company would mean there is demand for publicity on you; there is a demand to reach out to more people. You can create a Facebook page for your business just like Coca-Cola, which means you want to separate your business from your carrier. Like everything you do, whether you are writing a blog or creating a video, you want to have original content relevant to your audience, you want to use Facebook for some promotion, but every post does not necessarily need to be marketing your item or service. Looking at how the Coca-Cola page is strategized, it is not always only about the product; it is also about what they are doing for the community; this indicates that they are doing more community-based posts, and so to me, that's original content, positive content, a content that isn't necessarily pushing their product per, you could probably want to argue that "hey it's Coca-Cola" they have the biggest brand in the world, and that's true, but think about your product and services, think about your brand, if you're trying to build brand awareness, think about what your brand stands for and if your brand stands for say a global level impact, the ecosystem, the environment then, you probably want to be pushing outposts in that direction, if that's what you represent as a brand then you want people to know that because like-minded people are on Facebook and these like-minded people are going to be the ones who will like your page, who will also engage with your content and tell other people about it, so you always want to go regional you always want to be true to yourself and accurate to your brand, then you could take advantage of user-generated content like sharing a user's experience of using your product; in other terms, it would mean that if somebody is engaging with you or they have posted something about your brand and product, you can reciprocate, you can undoubtedly post something similar to what somebody's doing with your product or brand, that is an excellent way to create some original content by taking advantage of what the users have generated. Many more prominent brands have a more expansive space and community reviews. Now, if you are selling t-shirts, then hey, you can put something in there to help you sell that t-shirt, but Coca-Cola's strategy is hey what can we do to help build up our community, what can we do to fundraise so if we click on fundraise you can see they have.

Some of the things done on Facebook are posting polls, putting your Instagram feed in there, adding testimonials, getting creative, taking advantage of everything Facebook has to offer, and being true to yourself. Before you know it, you're going to start building up a community, gaining a reasonable amount of several likes on your business page, as well as some other tips. Now, for Facebook, when it comes to content you want to schedule your content, you don't want to just continue to post back-to-back you want to space your content out and another great advantage to Facebook as I already mentioned about social media marketing that's advertising so Facebook owns Instagram, they have a great tool for communicating called Facebook Messenger and so you can advertise leveraging Facebook messages you can leverage Instagram and what you need to do is if you go to Facebook's ad manager and you create a campaign when you go to create a campaign you are going click on placements and depending on what you are trying to do let us just say you are trying to build brand awareness you can actually hone in on you know Facebook you could hone in on Instagram you could do a number of different things within Facebook you have different ads available to you from single image ads to video ads to carousel see you have a lot of options and the biggest option on Facebook when it comes to advertising is your audience who are you targeting so remember Facebook has old young and everyone in between men and women and so you can specifically target interest you can specifically target gender and age allocation so Facebook really allows you to hone in on who your audience is if you're advertising and so that's the great thing about Facebook they have a lot of users and your you have an opportunity to hone in on a segment of that user base now Facebook also has metrics that you can look at to really understand how people are interacting with your ads how people are interacting with your post so let's take a look at that so if we go to Facebook when you go to your page you can click on insights and you can actually see some insights on posts that I've been posted on your page you can get insights into how many people viewed it how many people liked it how many people engaged how many people you reached with your post can you have information about videos followers Facebook provides recommendations so this is all part of Facebook Insights so if you're posting on Facebook Facebook will give you feedback as to how your post to perform it now if you're running ads on Facebook you can simply just view metrics related to how your ads are performing so you can see how many people clicked on an ad how many people the ad reached how much you've spent okay you can look at it by demographic you can even see cost per results so you can get a lot of good insights into how your ads are performing as well so if you're running a campaign targeting a specific audience on Facebook you can look at the you know stats and metrics surrounding that campaign and again for your Facebook page you have Facebook Insights so if you have any questions you know feel free we have a video called Facebook advertising tips and tricks so feel free to you know take a look at this video on simply learns YouTube channel for more information about facebook and if again if you have any comments to share about facebook feel free to put them under the comments section okay let's turn our attention to one of the platforms Instagram is owned by Facebook. so Instagram is a place where you can actually promote your brand product or service through the power of imagery or video and so the average number of monthly users on Instagram reaches 1 billion and 32% of all Internet users are on Instagram so a lot of users using it it's very easy platform use you just the only prerequisite you need your mobile phone so you open up that app it's as simple as just uploading an image that's what makes Instagram so popular, because it's just a simple tool to use. 60% of all Instagram users are women so unlike Facebook it does tend to slant more on the female side and 59% of the audience is a bit younger between age 18 to 29 so slants more women and Slim's more younger and so if these particular demographic and age groups tend to fit your target audience then Instagram is a place you probably want to be for social media marketing so as a magic content that works best our photos or videos I would always slant towards videos if you have them available but photos you know the rule of thumb is photos always tell a thousand words a thousand stories a thousand interpretations images are just always the best way to go as well I mean if you don't have the videos hey nothing to be sad about if you fall back on imagery so you can really put your brand in a good perspective and a good light by posting images and as you can imagine if 18 to 29 year old women are on Instagram you know that's skewing towards a certain demographic but in terms of industry it is open to most industries but the ones that tend to be most successful are beauty food and beverage and e-commerce no food beverage always tends to work well when you have video and imagery likewise beauty but ecommerce if you're selling that t-shirt or shoe you know Instagram allows the platform to work in a way where people can purchase that product right within the platform so that's why it tends to work well with e-commerce okay there are lots of channels just like on Facebook lots of channels on Instagram I mean some of the most followed brands are Chanel Starbucks Nike I mean If you have a product or service you'd like to promote, then Instagram is the way to go just for brand awareness if you're selling shoes then why not take images of and photos of their and get them posted on this to room like I said it's very simple to use all you need some hashtags to go along with that photo of a shoe or photo of that cup of coffee and Instagram kind of takes care of itself I mean photos do accentuate the product if you have them so leverage Instagram if you're really trying to build up some brand awareness for a particular product some best practices here on Instagram is you know have a compelling bio a good profile picture you know add a link to a landing page and you know leverage emojis if you have to so set yourself up nicely on Instagram you know if you're in a particular industry like food and beverage follow other food and beverage brands like coca-cola like Starbucks depends on what it is you really want to be related to so just make sure they're relevant get hashtags can't stress that enough you know when you post a photo throw some hashtags in there you can see what other people are hash tagging on Instagram and you can ride that wave of what's trending or you can create your own unique hashtag I'd probably have 2 to 3 hashtags per photo then don't be afraid to use both photos and videos videos do tend to work well on pretty much any platform they tend to work well on websites and blogs so why not use them on social media where people can engage ok so videos and imageries both work well on Instagram okay you can also get shoutouts from other influencers you plenty of influencers on Instagram especially in beauty especially in food and beverage fashion tends to be another industry that has a lot of influencers so feel free to reach out to them reciprocate see how you can work together where they can actually you know give you a shout-out on your particular product you want to keep your Instagram account updated you can update those with Instagram stories it's basically you showing off a particular product you know over a span of a few seconds or even a minute that's an Instagram story they're very popular easy to use you can even run contests to boost engagement so for example if your particular product is a particular food like a hamburger you know hey post a contest about you know allowing your followers to post the best good-looking tasty you know hamburger as an example or it could be something else in terms of fashion hey what's your best outfit on a Friday night before you go out for the evening you know there's always things you can do to spur engagement especially in a platform like Instagram where people like to post photos and then I mentioned this earlier with Facebook Ads you can run Instagram ads to give a particular post a boost so if we take a little snapshot of what we have available, you can choose from a variety of options in the Facebook Ads Manager, and probably also select Instagram as the particular platform so if you just want to advertise an Instagram when you go to your placements you could choose just Instagram either the feed or the stories so you can choose one of these two options if you wanted want to boost your posts get some more eyeballs on that it's a cost per click platform so anytime somebody clicks it's gonna cost you but you know just like Facebook you know the cost per click tends to slant a little bit lower it really depends on what you're trying to post when you're trying to post it who else is posting but hey the Instagram feed and the stories could be a good option if you're really trying to draw attention to a particular product let's turn our attention now to the b2b platform called LinkedIn LinkedIn is a very powerful popular business-to-business platform it has 260 million active users monthly and unlike Instagram where it Instagram slants more towards women LinkedIn slants more towards men 57% so a majority of the users are men but still you have a lot of women involved in on LinkedIn so a nice you know nice mix between both genders 38% of the user base are Millennials you know a lot of young people older people a nice mix from a business of different business segments different levels of business different business industries and verticals are on LinkedIn so don't be you know shying away from LinkedIn if your demographic or target audience tends to be older just because 38% are Millennials doesn't mean anything it means that everybody's using it it just that means that hey you know more than one-third of the users are Millennials are younger now LinkedIn is a b2b platform so if you're in the business of generating business leads then LinkedIn is the place for you to go there's opportunities for you to advertise on LinkedIn okay there's also opportunities for you to post lots of different content on LinkedIn so content that works on LinkedIn can be a blog it could be you know particular news article you know tips and best practices I've posted videos on LinkedIn you know it's good for jobs you said a lot of content on LinkedIn so please take a sneak peek at LinkedIn if I just go to LinkedIn here you know and I just go to my home the start news page you know I could see the types of content that's been posted so somebody just posted something with an image you know then you got an article down here okay you got you know an influencer like Richard Branson posting so you got a lot of different types of posts that you'll be able to see and you know leverage if you want to meaning when I say leverage you see somebody like Richard Branson posting something hey stay fit and healthy you know that's an image that's something about not about business per se but you know something interesting and unique so you can see all sorts of different types of content based on who you're following on LinkedIn and who you're connected to some things about LinkedIn you always want to create an engaging profile when I say engaging first things first make sure it's complete I mean there's lots of opportunities here. You also want to be able to post a lot of information about yourself, about what you're affiliated with, what jobs you've held, what groups you're associated with, what your interests are, what certifications you have. so you want to be able to complete your total profile. You can create a company page for your business. On LinkedIn, you can just search for simply learned and take a look at their business page, so if I just do a search for simply learn here. On

LinkedIn you want to make sure it's complete, you want to put information about the company, what jobs are available and you want your company to associate with that business page anybody who does you know follow that particular business page part of the organization is gonna be listed under people so and you want to be able to post just like on your personal profile if you have a business page you want to be able to post unique content I mean you can see here simply learn is posting you know some of the accolades that they have but they're taking that a step further they're also posting you know information about you know upcoming events and webinars so they're posting a mix of different content and that's ideally what you want to do on any social media platform is mix it up and just like you can on Facebook just like you can on Instagram you can you know boost a post per say okay so you can get that post in front of some additional eyeballs now of course you want to improve your company's web page for searches so it really does come down to how many people are following you but when you say when we say optimize your company page just make sure it's complete with some compelling content and then increase the number of followers you have so the great thing about LinkedIn that I like the most is that you know you can you know simply look at other people if I go back to say the home page you can actually see who's following what and you know LinkedIn does give you opportunities to connect with people okay so if I go to you if you go to your profile you'll be able to see other people that have viewed your particular page and you can connect with them pay or connect with people who are like-minded or similar or connected to people that you know so LinkedIn does a good job of presenting other people you can connect with so it makes it easier for you to increase the number of followers so having an engaging profile personal profile you know having an engaging company page making sure both your personal and the company page have all the content necessary have all of it completed and then increasing followers posting unique content I mean that's really the key to LinkedIn now again with LinkedIn you can use different media you can use videos SlideShare presentation images and you can boost content as I mentioned before you can boost content on LinkedIn so if you want to get that content in front of eyeballs you can do that so let's take a look at an example of a campaign and what you could do on LinkedIn in terms of sponsored content so if you go to LinkedIn's campaign manager I mean you have an opportunity put your ad in front of a particular audience so really depends again on who you're trying to target just like Facebook which slants more towards personal LinkedIn is gonna slant more towards business so with LinkedIn you have an opportunity to target a particular industry a particular company a particular job title okay so you could target everything business-related on LinkedIn so you can go ahead and create an ad the ads have imagery to support the ad and so basically when you set up your ad you set up your target you could choose your placement you're gonna be able to see you know who it is you're actually targeting and you can go ahead and great thing about LinkedIn is you have different ad formats and again you can get really creative with who you want to target and just like Facebook you know LinkedIn has you know some metrics that you can measure and figure out how your particular campaign performed by impressions buy click click the array even conversions cost per conversions and how many leads so LinkedIn has built in platform for measuring campaign success and so the differentiation between Facebook and LinkedIn is really this is the type of demographics that you have to choose from you know with LinkedIn you do have you know different options available based on business like your job title or job level or industry or vertical so you have a lot of examples available or a lot of options available to you on LinkedIn in terms of advertising okay let's talk about YouTube now so YouTube has 1.9 billion active users if it was a search engine it'd be the world's second-most-used search engine. The highest number of monthly active users in decreasing order starts at the United States Brazil Russia Japan and India all big markets all like to use YouTube but YouTube's popular across the world just like Facebook where the app is popular the app on for YouTube is very popular so 70% of all views are generated from mobile so with YouTube being a video platform you definitely need videos now there's a lot of industries on YouTube a lot of industries in some of the most successful brands on YouTube you know range from logo to coca-cola you know pretty much to every brand if you're a brand you want to be on YouTube because of the massive reach that YouTube has to offer coupled with video and how great video is in terms of engagement it's a just a great combination okay so some best practices here for YouTube you want to optimize your video for SEO to get views and so we have a video that we've created at simply learn how to rank YouTube videos so if you watch that video you'll get some really good tips and strategies about how to you know optimize your video for youtube the very least you want to make sure that you're using right the right keywords and the title description and hashtags so that's a start when we talk about optimizing your videos want to upload regularly and fix the schedule for your videos because if you're starting to get followers on YouTube or subscribers they're gonna expect you to produce more video especially if you're producing engaging unique relevant content for that target audience so we're not saying you have to have a video once a day or once a week start small and build up and get on a regular schedule and then you can organize your videos in a playlist so you know if we look at simply learn you simply learn does a good job of organizing their videos into a playlist so all you have to do is go to simply learn YouTube channel and see how it's broken down into playlists now YouTube also has the ability because it is global you do have the ability to provide translations so if your target audience is from another country it probably wouldn't be a bad idea like Facebook and Instagram or like LinkedIn you can advertise on YouTube you would just need to do that through Google Ads so with Google Ads you're gonna say Google I want to advertise and YouTube and you have plenty of available options to available to you anything from you know pre-roll to showing up in the middle of a video to showing up you know before or at the conclusion of a video all the way to native content marketing where you know your ad is showing up next to a video so you've plenty of options for advertising on YouTube and then just like an Instagram there are our influencers on YouTube you know feel free to reach out to these influencers and see if you can collaborate in some way where maybe you post their video on your channel they post your video on their channel and vice versa so you want to be able to maybe collaborate somehow to get some views on your video okay let's talk about Twitter now so with Twitter is a micro blogging platform and so when I say micro blogging I mean limited in characters limited in how much you can actually post but it's very popular it has 326 million active users per month and it does tend to slant a lot towards Millennials it's a lot of young people use Twitter and a lot of people use it to get their news so no longer are the days of grabbing that newspaper no longer the days of going maybe to a media news site online you can quickly go to Twitter and get all your news right there in a feed an easy feed let's take a peek at Twitter here you know I can get everything from you know somebody posting something specific about their dog you know all the way to a particular job you know all the way to industry news you know all the way to basically an advertisement all the way to a specific news article so it's all here on Twitter in your feed so Twitter does offer videos so videos do work well so if I go back here you can see you know here's a video of Antonio Brown he's posting a video of his news conference and another promotional video so industries that capitalize on Twitter as you can guess if a lot of people go there from their news you probably see a lot of news and media and entertainment on Twitter so that doesn't necessarily mean that you can't use Twitter for your brand it really comes down to target audience some of the most influential brands are slanted more towards you know news and media but you know you got cosmetics you got gaming companies you're gonna everybody's on Twitter okay it just comes down to does this platform have your target audience and given the nature Twitter you know how can you get your particular brand product or service out there in so many character okay some other advantages and best practices you can use on Twitter so I would recommend implementing Twitter cards and all Twitter cards does is allow you to attach rich photographs or videos to tweets, as well as different media experiences. When you can attach rich media like videos and images to tweets, it can help drive traffic and engagement to your website. With just a few lines of markup added to your web page, users who tweet links to your content will see a quote-unquote card appear in the tweet that is visible to their followers. So, that's how it works I would certainly look to get Twitter cards implemented if you are going to use Twitter as your platform of choice for social media marketing so it does enhance the experience for the end user and because allows you as an advertiser or as somebody leveraging social media to really enhance your tweet and it just provides a better experience for the end user who's looking at your tweet and so like LinkedIn you can really take a look at who's trending what's trending on so Twitter makes it easy for you to you know follow so here they'll list of who to follow so these who to follow are similar to what you've been posting or similar to your industry and then here you can look at trends you can look at what hashtags are trending and so if you click on a particular hashtag you can you know follow a particular you know person who or organization who tweeted something so you always are reminded in Twitter who to follow and so it makes it easier for you to pick and choose who to follow and build up your following fairly quickly because Twitter actually provides you with opportunities on who to follow just like LinkedIn just like YouTube just like Instagram there are influencers out there people who have a large number of followers who tweet on a regular basis who tweet original content who get high engagement these are influencers and these are the people you want to engage with so look for those people on Twitter follow them I mean the rule of thumb is if you follow someone on Twitter you know generally they're gonna follow you back so if you can engage and follow influencers you have an opportunity to see not only what they're tweeting but the ability to communicate with them and engage with them as an influencer so maybe they can retweet one of your tweets and get that tweet out in front of their followers so you can advertise on Twitter and the unique thing about advertising on Twitter you can you promote your tweet just like you promote a post on Facebook or Instagram or LinkedIn but more so I think than any other platform is the use of hashtags and so use appropriate relevant hashtags I always tend to use a unique hashtag but also depends on what you're tweeting about if there's something that's trending and again Twitter will tell you what's trending in terms of hashtags if it's something you're tweeting about then go ahead and use that

Tash tag as well you can have multiple hashtags in a particular tweet and so don't be afraid to use the unique hashtag with a hashtag that's trending because the whole idea is you want your tweet to get noticed and then you can use tweet chat or some there's some other tools out there that are available to allow you to find people to follow and these people may be interested in your product or service because you believe they will appeal to your target market, or you can network with like-minded people in the same business or who sell similar goods or interests so tweet shots available for that reason and you want to take advantage of these tools because again with Twitter it's easy to build a following but you want to build a following that is going to engage with your tweets so let's talk about what tools are available for social media marketing so when we talk about all these platforms available to us okay we talk about Facebook and Instagram and we talked about LinkedIn and Twitter and YouTube I mean those are popular platforms but at the beginning of the session I mentioned there's hundreds of social media platforms out there and if you're posting content on a number of them you want to be able to organize that content you want to be able to organize it and schedule it you know where it makes sense and when it makes sense you want to stay organized and so there are tools available to help you stay organized tools like HootSuite buffer or sprout social okay some of these tools are available you know at a cost of a free trial or at a low cost per month so regardless of whether you're using a free version of one of these tools or another tool mint listed or you're actually paying for it it's worth the investment if you're going to partake and social media marketing and even if you're on one platform it's still worth it to have a social media tool available to help you schedule and not only do these social media tools help you schedule they do a lot of other things too for example they help you measure the engagement of your posts so let's say example of one of them like sprout social so if I go to sprout social here I can see for a particular company I'm able to see you know how my post and get we're engaged okay so I could see daily engagements on particular platforms I can also you know schedule my post so I can go ahead and pick a time and date to schedule them and so I can go ahead and post something and put it in a queue to be published for example tomorrow or next week or whatever the case may be so these tools do a lot for you I mean they help you discover new followers they give you in-depth reports they help you stay organized and so to me it's worth the investment to look at one of the tools listed here you know these are some of the more popular ones - maybe even a free version but regardless of how much you pay and what tool you're using it's still worth the investment just to make sure you're scheduling your post at the appropriate time so you're not posting something back-to-back as an example and you're able to measure accordingly so it's nice to be able to go into a tool like sprout social go to reports and measure you know in one place you know how Twitter is performing or how Facebook is performing or how LinkedIn is performing and so that's what's a lot of these tools provide is nice reporting options and nice scheduling options so you can find more content you can create by using these tools again you can schedule efficiently analyze them and you can use insights to improve your campaign so why these tools give you nice insights to how the post was actually engaged and you want to be able to leverage that and some of these tools if not all of them have social listening and social listening is monitoring what's being posted out there so what else is posted you can take a look at and if it's something interesting or relevant you can go ahead and follow or take part in that conversation okay so that's what social listening allows you to do and a lot of these platforms have that as a feature so let's take a look at tips to be a good social media marketer so some of the important things you should take care of our set up a social media marketing plan when I say set up a social media marketing plan there's some questions you want to be able to ask okay what platforms am I gonna use what's my objective on each platform in fact before you choose the platform you want to figure out what your objective is in terms of social media so your objective could be different on each platform it could be brand awareness on Facebook and it could be promoting a particular product on Twitter your objective is gonna be on each platform you want to be able to choose your KPIs and align your KPIs with each platform meaning you'll need to determine what metrics are relevant to your business goals and what kind of material you'll post on different social media networks, so you'll need to get organized and put a plan in place and then you want to create informative shareable actionable and relevant content and what I mean by all that is you want to create unique content that doesn't mean you can't leverage what other people are doing meaning you know if I'm you know in the shoe business I can certainly go to Nike or adidas or puma or Reebok and see what kind of posts they're putting out and then I could take their cue and do something similar but I want it to be unique to me and I want it to be unique to my brand and I want to be able to keep my content visual meaning I want to be able to use as many photos and videos as I can that's available to me because remember videos generate better engagement I want to be active and responsive with my customer base meaning the whole point of social media is to engage and people are going to respond they're gonna comment they're going to take part in what you post and so whatever they do you want to be able to respond accordingly whether that's positive or negative and then you want to measure metrics like conversion rates and click the rate so that goes back to putting a plan in place figure out what your metrics are and then when you're posting on a particular platform you want to be able to lean on those metrics to make sure you're achieving your goals so you want to have those metrics in place beforehand and then you want to be able to use those metrics moving forward as you post the whole idea is if you're measuring what you post you're obviously going to want to lean more towards what's working versus what's not working.

Chapter Two

The Insta-Marketing Strategy: Instagram Marketing Strategy

Instagram, a quirky and engaging image-sharing software, has taken the world by storm since October 2010. Hundreds of millions of Instagram users use filters and frames to turn ordinary photos and videos into memories shared with the rest of the world. Instagram is almost likely a good place to look for photographs and videos of your business. This material serves as genuine peer-to-peer recommendations of your company, which is effectively free promotion. You can only assist in compounding this impact by implementing a strong plan of your own, building brand loyalty, and generating sales as a consequence. Many people have even referred to Instagram as "The World's Most Powerful Selling Tool," such as the amount of enthusiasm shown by its members.

These individuals are under the age of thirty, are engaged, and many of them are consumers.

Understand the "Culture of Instagram" and how it works.

The top-performing companies on Instagram all have one thing in common: they understand what distinguishes the app from additional social networking sites and how to take advantage of this understanding to increase their reach and sales. The notion of "Instagram culture" will undoubtedly evolve, but at its heart, users are proud of the material they create and share with the world - you won't find hundreds of impetuous selfies and hazy nightclub shots from the most successful "artists," for example. As a result, designers place significant priority on quality rather than quantity. With creators devoting significant time to meticulously compose and construct photos and videos, cropping and editing until they are perfect, so that when an item is finally posted to their Instagram feed, it is gushed over by delighted followers, complemented by a flurry of likes and comments, and attracts new followers in the process. One of Instagram's most popular slogans is "discover beauty everywhere," encouraging users to look for beauty everywhere they go. To achieve this, companies must demonstrate their worldview through imagery that goes beyond the common perception of them, as well as provide a glimpse into the lifestyle that your product or service makes possible, both through your own eyes and those of customers who use your products or services. Overall, while visual imagery for social media platforms like Facebook and Twitter may occasionally be more ad-hoc in nature, and Pinterest may be more simple and mood board-y or sales, your preference on Instagram should be more creative, arty, and special. It would help if you placed even more emphasis on visual storytelling, turning ordinary situations into artistic moments, and capturing the essence of your brand throughout. Make it a point to become immersed in the culture of Instagram by including more imaginative photos or videos in your feed (which clearly expresses a defined personality and voice as well as mirroring the attitude or preferences of the majority audience), and you'll be in a significantly powerful position from the start.

What are the qualities of a high-quality Instagram photograph, and how do you create one? As you are now aware, just putting any old picture into Instagram will not cut it with the app's sophisticated audience; you must be much more creative and discriminating in your posting. Talking about discovering what kind of photographs Instagram wants firms to publish to keep customers happy, one of the greatest places to start is by looking at its suggestions for Instagram ads: There is no excessive use of picture filters as a means of masking the "truth" of a photo, and no use of text overlays is permitted. Brands are not permitted to use their logo in Instagram advertisements unless it is a natural and unobtrusive setting element. Images used in advertisements must be "authentic to your brand," which means they must not be surprising or corny, and they must not use gimmicks. Photos for advertisements should depict "moments" rather than things. In other words, advertisements must be more than simply a photograph of your goods; they must be something unique and exciting. Ads should use ideas and signals from the current Instagram community, particularly popular hashtags, to be effective. Continue to keep these principles at heart as you go through the remainder of the chapter's guidance and consider how you want to structure your own Instagram strategy.

In the same way that a lot of social media theory doesn't apply to every circumstance all of the time, these principles might serve as a good foundation for your activity. It's very fantastic stuff. By the way, there's a ton more material and strategy for Instagram advertisements available on the internet.

Instagram Profile Optimization is important. Create a profile picture suitable for a circle in your Instagram bio and optimize your bio.

One of the simplest and most efficient ways to communicate with potential followers is to optimize your Instagram bio. Give folks a cause to follow you by describing what sets you apart, remind them that they'll be among the first to know about special offers and promotions, first to get a sneak peek at new product lines, and first to enter Instagram competitions; use the complete 150-character limit for a chance to win great prizes. Do not forget to include the URL to your website in your bio area as well — this is the only location on Instagram where a link will be clickable and visible to others. Maintain a light and amusing tone while using relevant keywords (SEO), an Emoji if the mood strikes you, and a business-specific hashtag, among other things. In an interesting twist, many businesses are deliberately choosing to comprise a link to their blog rather than a link to their online store, demonstrating how they view Instagram as an opportunity to gradually build their brand image as a whole rather than "force" people into making a purchase right away. If you are the company's face, it is also critical to add a photo or profile of yourself (preferably with a cheerful look) or your corporate logo since this will serve as your company's official representation throughout the service. For the same reason as Google+, Instagram (at least on its mobile version) prefers a circular profile picture, which complements people's faces more than corporate logos.

Post only your finest photographs, and get inspiration from other people's work. The most significant companies on Instagram are incredibly selective about the images they put on their accounts. Quality, rather than quantity, is paramount for your portfolio on Instagram. It is essential that you take your time in assembling a collection of images that you are pleased with and that represents your finest work since it is this that will attract readers' attention both when seen as individual pieces of content and when browsing through your gallery as a whole. Many of the most well-known firms on Instagram only post once or twice a day, sometimes even less often. Here are a few basic photography concepts and recommendations to help you enhance the overall value of your Instagram work: Photos on Instagram have traditionally been squares – similar to an old Polaroid photograph – This is still the most common layout technique on Instagram nowadays. Before the shutter of your widescreen camera view is closed, attempt to visualize how your design would seem like a square once the sides have been cropped. When it comes to

Instagram photos, the 'rule of thirds' is firmly embedded in many of the best ones. However, when there is a key aspect of your material that a court will annoyingly clip out, the same goes for other kinds of photography. Imagine that your viewfinder has been divided into thirds, horizontally and vertically (or that you have turned on the iPhone Camera grid view through the Options menu); now, balance your composition between these three sections. Obtain symmetrical photos that appear fantastic on Instagram and other social media platforms. You'll be left with a perfectly square crop of your picture at the end of the process. When taking a snapshot, the essential thing to keep in mind is is to keep yourself centered and ensure that all of your lines are completely straight. Make use of angles and lines to your advantage. Instagram is about enabling its users to see the world in new ways. Everyone is used to seeing the world from head height, so try shooting from high and low perspectives, as well as from behind and to the side, to add interest and excitement to your photographs.

Additionally, consider including lines into your photographs - whether they are natural components such as a line of trees or a road that stretches into the distance - to pull people's attention into the picture or towards whatever it is that you want them to see. Do practice concentrating on specific aspects of items or services to attract clients, rather than blander long or mid-range photos to make the most of the comparatively little real estate available on mobile devices (where most of your Instagram material will be seen). The quality dye and material in a garment may be highlighted in a clothes store's advertisement, while a decorating business would choose something more abstract and utilize the close-up view of paint and brush to indicate a job well done. Look for sources of inspiration. If you're having trouble staying inspired, check out Instagram's Explore page (the compass points symbol) to observe the newest developing trends on the platform and try incorporating them into your work practices.

Consistent filters and image editing helps to distinguish your photographs. Instagram's popularity has soared in part due to the simplicity with which users can change regular images into something extraordinary with the app's vintage filters. While these overlays continue to be a key part of the app's appeal, the app's image editing tools have evolved in response to competition to include a variety of additional options for photo tweaking, such as straightening, lux, brightness, contrast, tilt-shift, sharpening, and other effects. With a simple slider, Instagram enables you to control the intensity of each of the adjustments. Overall, I'd recommend subtly applying them (to align with Instagram's preferred approach for brands, which is natural) and selecting a filter that you will use consistently; one that helps the image to reflect your brand culture and personality (e.g., fun, playful, serious, professional), and one that makes your style instantly recognizable within the feed of your fans. Filters may play an essential part in developing a unique branded Instagram account, learning what your followers enjoy about you, and creating consistent material with that theme.

Consider capturing your images on a different platform besides Instagram. If you take a picture inside Instagram, you are immediately obligated to use the app's filters and editing tools to modify it. Despite how many these choices have gotten, it is frequently preferable to take a shot using the built-in camera software on your smartphone (or any other digital camera). If you follow these steps, you will have a 'clean' picture that can be loaded into any photo editing product you like after that (VSCO Cam or Afterlight, for instance - tools that may provide a more unique and diverse filter and image editing options). After that, you may import the picture into Instagram for final editing before uploading it when you're through with it; this is how the experts can create such stunning photographs, which are incomparably different from anything that can be produced alone on Instagram. Of course, if Instagram currently gives you the appearance and feel that you like for your images, that is also acceptable!

Instagram Marketing and Content Plan; Make the most of the picture caption that appears alongside every image on Instagram - It's a small but essential part of your marketing plan. - and never leave it blank. Instagram Marketing and Content Strategy; Make use of it to anchor the substance of the image and convey your company's personality and tone of voice. Examples of utilizing the picture caption include a description of the product you're promoting, asking a question, or initiating a debate, including a call to action and a URL you want your followers to see. Because

URLs published inside Instagram descriptions cannot be clicked on, make sure they are short and memorable and use a site like bit.ly to help you with this if needed. Referencing the previous point, another common approach to drive clickthroughs from Instagram captions to your chosen location is adding a sentence such as "click the link in our bio" in the caption. Because your bio is constantly accessible with a single touch, and because the "Website" URL there is currently live, it will save folks the time and effort of opening up a new browser and manually putting in a URL, if that is their choice.

Unlike other social media platforms, Instagram captions do not have a character restriction. For certain businesses, such as National Geographic, this technique results in captions that read like mini-magazine articles. Combining it with high-quality photographs allows viewers to get more engrossed in their material for a longer period, allowing them to experience them as more than just snapshots. Do you need to update a caption to fix an error or add more detail? Select "Edit" from the drop-down menu that appears next to your picture.

Don't be spammy with your hashtagging; instead, follow the latest trends. When you include #hashtags in your Instagram captions, the material will be paired alongside other photographs with the same hashtag and made into clickable links to the photosets containing the content. Because hashtags can be used to find content on Instagram, making use of the appropriate hashtags might assist you in getting your content in front of individuals who are looking for keywords and phrases linked with your company (words in your description that are not preceded with a hashtag will not be taken into account when a user searches). Assuring that your hashtags accurately describe your content will make it easier for visitors to locate you. General hashtags such as #clothing or #food may bring in a few new followers, but they're also quite popular, and your material may get lost in the shuffle when people search for them. Using more precise and descriptive hashtags will give you a far higher chance of getting discovered and followed. For a different approach, whole Instagram communities may be developed around a single actionable, custom-created hashtag - and this is a strategy that works across all social media platforms. Create a hashtag connected to your brand and use it to bring consumers together. Please encourage them to use the hashtag and reward them with likes and comments when they do. Study the most popular hashtags within your company area and include them in your approach. It would help if you also tried using popular but not overused hashtag trends on Instagram to help define your content. Among the most popular of these are #thingsorganizedneatly (a topdown photo of several related items, such as a full outfit or multi-piece toolset, organized in a manner that is pleasing to the eye; often compounded by the use of complementary colors), #fromwhereistand (a first-person, top-down photo of a person's feet, with an emphasis on footwear and the ground below to tell a story), #onthetable (elegant top-down photos of (marking the end of the week with an eyecatching symmetrical scene from your store, city, or elsewhere). While browsing Instagram, you will note how over-the-top hashtag use can be, especially considering that each picture or video may only include a maximum of 30 hashtags. Although this generous limit helps people - who are frequently anxious for an audience - garner a few different views, I would not advocate using such an obvious strategy for commercial purposes since it might come off as spammy, dilute your marketing message, and harm your brand's reputation. Trackman, a competition analysis business, discovered that utilizing between 4 and 5 hashtags boosted Instagram engagements but that using more than five hashtags decreased engagement on the platform. More than three hashtags in each post, similar to what is done on Twitter, in my opinion, will make the content appear crowded.

On Instagram, you can geotag your photos with the location where they were taken. (with the help of a small technique), and these photos are then put on a Photo Map. When a picture is tagged in this manner, Instagrammers who are nearby or who visit your area at a later time will be able to see your images and interact with them. In turn, this affinity may result in a follow or a visit to your business, and it usually enhances the feeling of location and interest in the photograph. If your company's goal is to reach customers in a certain geographic location, the Places search page may assist you in accomplishing that goal. Related: You may utilize the Top and Most Recent posts from any place to interact with them, and you can use the material you see as inspiration for producing the sort of content popular with people in a given area.

Other people's images are being "programmed." There is no healthier method to attract new consumers to your business than to exhibit photos of existing customers who value what you have to offer. Ask for images to be provided to you by satisfied customers, or - even better - use particular hashtags to search them out on social media. When you discover a photograph you like, use an app like Regram for iOS or PhotoRepost for Android to share it on your social media page. Don't forget to tag the person who originally shot the photo so that they are aware that you used their image. Customers' doodles are often included on the Sharpie website, while Starbucks "piggybacks" on the popularity of Instagram users that have big follow bases by publishing photographs (with permission, of course) that contain their goods.

Chapter Three
Tik-Tok

TikTok has grown worldwide, and many retailers now receive visitors from TikTok. It is not difficult to generate traffic from a platform during its first stages. As a result, it is critical for each seller to have effective TikTok marketing techniques in place to increase their following and traffic.

Conduct Your Research

Without a doubt, studying and getting exceptional information about your area remains critical to success. The first step is to gather as much information as possible about your closest competitors. You must understand the content they produce and deduce the specifics of their success from their videos; this may be challenging, but it is worthwhile to take cautious measures. When you investigate them, you may notice that they make specific errors. You can differentiate yourself by filling a void and doing things differently.

Produce Useful And Creative Content

One of the most enjoyable methods to discover what we like on social media is through videos, which have grown in popularity in recent years. However, to successfully engage our audience and market our business, we must develop valuable and creative videos. In this manner, we can maintain the interest of our fans. Our video appears to be engaging to capture their attention and provide value to our users. Make use of your imagination. Remember that individuals use social media to entertain themselves, so avoid uploading videos that dull the viewer.

Build Partners

If you are committed to operating your business independently, there may be occasions when collaboration with others is unavoidable. If you connect with someone in a similar industry, you can exchange ideas. You could alter one action you have never carried out before and completely transform your traffic. They may also pick up some helpful information from you.

Maintain Consistency

TikTok is the entertainment king, so do everything it takes to assure regular updates and consistency with your TikTok videos, just as you would with a blog.

Increase Your Followers' Engagement. How do you accomplish this? Here are some excellent suggestions:

Submit A Question: It's simple to ask questions about your audience, for instance. How do you feel about the cold weather? This type of inquiry will instill a sense of commitment and affection in them, encouraging them to watch your videos religiously. That is the type of marketing required. Therefore, ask open inquiries frequently.

Invite Your Followers To Vote: Include your audience in the process by presenting them with options; when they reply, you will have already committed them. Allow them to select their position on contentious life problems; this is beneficial because it will stimulate debate. Never take a side with any of your followers. Allow them to discuss matters independently while you serve as moderator.

Make Your Posts During Your Fans' Online Time: Conduct research and determine your fans' internet activity. Thus, by releasing your videos, you will increase your viewership.

Interact With Other Brands: This is highly beneficial since it enables you to market your business to a population that your business never could reach on its own, and a portion of the traffic produced will result in sales. It would be beneficial if you kept in mind that you must share beneficial stuff here.

Crowdsource Comments: You need comments to remain visible to your audience; this is how you'll determine if they enjoy your material or not. One advantage is that individuals have no difficulty validating the comments. It would help if you approached them positively. It would be beneficial if you asked questions to respond to honestly. For instance, where should you focus your next contest's improvements? Will your audience be quick to provide meaningful feedback?

TikTok is very prominent among its end users, yet it can be perplexing and challenging to navigate for people new to it. TikTok is a spin-off of Musical.ly, a platform for social media where users could record themselves lip-syncing to audio snippets, and then the videos are subsequently shared with their pals. To put it simply, It's a video-based app that lets you watch and share videos either by making videos within the application or by posting videos from your mobile. So, why should you be interested in

TikTok? How about a billion downloads and installations? That's a significant number of folks who are utilizing the app.

However, aside from its scrolling video feed, there aren't many similarities between TikTok and the Vine app of the same age. TikTok differs from Vine because it is based on concise, six-second films, whereas Vine is more structured. This independence has resulted in various forms and memes that have cropped up on the platform, ranging from quick doodles to DIY photography lessons. As users download the app, more businesses are flocking to it in the hopes of capitalizing on this game-changing platform for marketing purposes. TikTok is primarily a video-based social media site. The app's unique video editing features include filters, music, transitions, unique animations, graphics, and other video editing capabilities. Essential editing functions allow you to tap into your video-making abilities even if you have never used video-editing software before using these functions. Furthermore, similar to other micro-blogging networks, the brief format makes it simple to post and consume the website.

You must be familiar with lingo to comprehend TikTok. To get you started, a few key terms to familiarize yourself with the app are highlighted below:

For You Page: This is the app's home page, where you can find all of its features. For You is a TikTok website that displays a selection of videos that have been hand-picked for you based on your prior viewing history. Following an initial assessment of the types of videos you enjoy, TikTok's algorithm will serve up recommended videos (by grouping together related videos) to each user based on their preferences. Your initial stop on TikTok is the For You page, but like with any platform, if you dig a bit further, you'll discover lively communities based on specific interests.

The Discover Page is where you'll find new content that has been shared on TikTok. The Discover page provides content based on themes, hashtags, viral videos, and other criteria... This is the starting point for exploring the content beyond the For You page.

This is the app section, where you'll find content from the individuals you're following on the platform.

Challenges: The TikTok experience is not complete without the presence of challenges. In this section, creators improve on a video concept created by another user, giving it its own unique touch and flair.

Duets: Duets occur between authors, and you'll find examples of them all around the app, including the home screen. Duets allow other content creatives to work on the contents of other users.

If you're not familiar with the term, a hashtag is a keyword phrase used to classify and aggregate material on social media platforms. Hashtags are incredibly crucial to TikTok's culture and algorithm, and they are used extensively.

What are the marketing advantages of TikTok?

Using the TikTok application for brand promotion, there are three options available to businesses:

To begin, the user can build their own channel and add videos that they believe are related to their interests.

Second, the user can collaborate with influential individuals to assist their material get shared more broadly over the internet.

Third, the customers can pay for TikTok marketing. However, the platform does not have the same reach as YouTube in terms of audience. Over time, it may, on the other hand, gain in popularity and stability.

In general, many brands mix their own channels and collaborate with influential persons to reach a broader audience with the content of their products. Furthermore, they can experiment with other concepts on their own channels, such as hashtag challenges, user-generated content, and TikTok advertising.

It is also possible for users to recommend to their influencers that they distribute this type of material in their networks.

Chapter Four
Facebook: The Ultimate marketing strategy

Facebook is the most popular social network globally, with over a billion users on desktop and mobile. Your target audience will undoubtedly be present because you are the undisputed king of social media. Utilize these techniques to develop, promote, and market your business on Facebook, resulting in an engaged following.

Strategy for Creating a Facebook Business Page Before you plunge in and begin posting on Facebook, It's a smart option to lay some solid foundations for your brand presence so that it's ready to inspire men when they come across your page. Let's start on the road to making your Facebook page a destination worth visiting regularly.

Establish a Facebook Page rather than a personal profile. When you sign up on Facebook, you are automatically assigned a Personal Timeline. Personal Timelines, also known as profiles, are intended for personal, non-commercial usage. While Facebook Pages resemble personal Timelines, they give brands unique resources such as analytics, specific tabs for business-related content, and advertising opportunities. Pages are not required to have a separate Facebook account and do not require a different login from Timelines. A Facebook Page can be created through one of three main ways: by typing 'Create A Page' into the site's search box at the top, by clicking the 'Create A Page' button at the top of any existing Facebook Page, or by clicking the 'Create A Page' button at the top of any current Facebook Page.

If you presently utilize a personal Timeline for business reasons, Facebook may discover and terminate your account without notice. To offer you an opportunity to fix this blunder, Facebook has created a tool that will convert your Timeline to a business Page. When you convert your account to a Facebook Page, your current profile image is maintained, and all of your profile's friends are restored to "like" fans of your Page. Additionally, the username linked with your account will become the identifier of your Page, and the name associated with your account will become the identifier of your Page (you may be able to change this if you wish - I explain how in the next tip). Other content, including wall postings, photographs, and videos, will not be moved over to your new Page, so make sure to download a backup of this data (via your profile settings) if you wish to retain it. If you use your profile for both personal and commercial purposes, the simplest method to avoid getting in trouble is to suspend any business activity on your Timeline, build a separate business page, and then encourage your audience to unfriend your account and "like" your new business account. While a Facebook Page is essential for businesses on Facebook, an individual Timeline offers a variety of non-commercial options to engage with customers and clients on a more personal level.

Maintain a concise Facebook Page name; Make sure you get it correctly the first time!

If feasible, keep your Facebook Page name short since this will aid in creating Facebook advertising, where the headline space (which is frequently your Page's name) is limited to just 25 characters. You can manually modify the name of a Facebook Page if it has fewer than 200 likes, so choose wisely early on. Navigate to the "About" tab beneath your Page's cover photo if you are dissatisfied with the name of your platform as it is changeable. Save by clicking "Edit" next to the Name section. Changing the name of your Page has no effect on its username or web URL (explained below).

Create a unique web address for your Facebook Page.

For your Facebook Profile, create a temporary URL. (available once you reach 25 likes), preferably one named after your brand; this will make it much easier to direct visitors to your Facebook Page. Consider this carefully since you will only be able to modify this URL once in the future (through the "About" tab); otherwise, you will be forced to erase your Page and start again - not ideal if you have a sizable fan base! To quickly achieve the 25-fan mark, invite your email contacts and current Facebook friends - a group of people who are already invested in you and your brand - to visit and "Like" your Page via the "Promote" drop-down menu at the top of your Facebook Page.

Complete the business information accurately and completely.

Fill in as much information about your company as possible in the About section of your Facebook Page, including the address, contact information, product information, website (use commas to separate multiple URLs in the website box), and links to other social media sites. Customers benefit from your efforts to populate these portions since they consolidate your key information in one place. The keyword-rich blurb is also appropriate for (SEOs), as Google indexes the language in your About section. Are you the restaurant owner, and have you chosen the restaurant/cafe category for your Page? Include the types of items you serve and publish your menu as a PDF for customers to browse; alternatively, if you're in the United States or Canada, you can add a menu using SinglePlatform. Nota bene: Depending on how your Page is classified, the first-viewed section of the About section may appear differently on the Facebook mobile app than it does on the desktop version. It will display your Short Description to some mobile users, your Mission to others, and a piece of your entire Company Description to yet others. With this in mind, it may be prudent to update each of these elements, beginning with your website URL, to ensure that it is always the first thing mobile consumers see.

Verify your Page and add an official checkmark to your profile picture.

If your business has a physical address in the real world, Facebook allows you to verify your Page and add an official grey checkmark to its cover photo, similar to the blue checkmark given to celebrities and other famous entities. To authenticate your Page, go to the Page Settings menu and pick Verify Page from the General section. To validate your company representative status, you must contact a publicly listed business phone number or upload an official document, such as a business phone or utility bill, business license, or business tax file. It's well worth the work because Verified Pages rank higher in search results and show users right away that you're the official brand page for your firm on Facebook.

Create an eye-catching cover image and include a call-to-action button.

Because Facebook Page cover photographs can be seen by most people on the platform, it makes the most of the space by successfully communicating your brand or message in a single, high-quality image. The ideal size is 851 315 pixels; any less and Facebook will stretch the image, resulting in a fuzzy appearance. Cover photo ideas include a single strong image that communicates who you are and what you do, a collage of your products, highlighting an ongoing promotion, or featuring a photo or testimonial submitted by one of your fans - the latter will truly "wow" your customer, and hopefully, encourage them to tell their friends. Maintain user engagement by altering your cover photo and profile picture regularly - once a month is an ideal target, but seasonal changes are also popular with firms.

Fundamentals of Facebook Marketing

Now that your Facebook Page looks beautiful and you're encouraging people to visit it let's look at some strategies to maximize its effectiveness.

Affix significant posts

For up to a week, You can pin a single post to the top of your Page's Timeline on Facebook. Use this to draw attention to important content and boost the number of people that visit your Page. All new status updates will show beneath the pinned post until it is unpinned (or a week has passed), at which point it will revert to its chronological order. Following creating a post, hover over it until the pencil icon appears, then click it and select 'Pin to Top.' Consider pinning posts that contain special announcements, material, or promotions.

Repost high-quality information, but avoid becoming spammy in your approach.

Given that not everyone checks their Facebook News Feed every day and that only a tiny fraction of your fans will see your material the first time if you have a good article or link to offer, share it multiple times to ensure that as many of your people as possible see it. However, make a concentrated attempt to communicate the information in various ways, for example, by different language in the text, an image with a link, or a link-sharing post. While image-based posts with links are worth experimenting with, standard link-share seats are frequently advised since they mirror how the average user uses Facebook; when was the last time you saw a friend share a link with an uploaded image? Facebook will punish your reach if you frequently publish the same status, as it has discovered that people dislike "copy and paste" updates.

Utilize call-to-actions to increase clicks but prevent "click-baiting."

To increase click-through rates from Facebook and other social media platforms to your website and blog, being precise about what you want your clients to do via a clear call to action is frequently a solid option, e.g., "Click here for additional information [your link]." Frequently, that slight push is all that separates a successful status from one that vanishes without a trace.

Ensure views by utilizing the "Get All Notifications" and "See First" strategies.

One strategy for ensuring that all of your Page's content is seen by all of your fans is to train them to select the "Get Notifications" and "See First" choices located in a drop-down menu when hovering their cursor over the "Liked" and "Following" buttons beneath your Page's cover photo. When this option is selected, whenever you publish a new status update, the fans in question will receive an alert via the blue "globe" icon in their Facebook account's status bar, and your new material will show at the top of that user's News Feed. These requests are best expressed via a status update accompanied by a menu screenshot demonstrating the desired action. It's totally up to you whether you feel at ease asking at the risk of appearing pushy, and your decision should be based on the quality of your relationship with your audience. If you choose to do so, I will not frequently force it on followers, primarily because they are unlikely to be on your Page when your instructions appear and are even less likely to click through and follow-through.

Alternate between videos published on ed on YouTube and those shared on Facebook.

The advent of video content on Facebook has altered the social media environment, and it will continue to do so. Often, it makes sense to upload compelling video content directly to the site instead of sharing a YouTube link; this is because the native Facebook video receives a more equitable distribution of reach (but keep an eye on your analytics to see how things go). If the video is "evergreen" in nature (i.e., It will continue to be as vital in the future as it is now.), why do you need to broadcast it twice - once directly to Facebook and again via a shared YouTube link? Strategies for maximizing the impact of videos submitted to Facebook include having them play automatically – and without audio – within the News Feed. With that in mind, consider how you'll entice fans to watch your clip (and turn on the sound) from the very first frame – catching their eye with movement in the first 2-3 seconds is one way, or if a person is seen speaking in front of the camera, fans who are interested will click to hear what's being said. Using the Video tab on your Page, organize videos into playlists (to encourage increased watch time), and select one video to Feature. The Featured video will feature in a prominent place below the "About" section of your Page's sidebar - a fantastic opportunity to showcase your business or promote a current promotion. Tag individuals who appear in your films, add relevant captions and choose the best thumbnail from the option that displays once the file is posted (or upload your custom image). Additionally, don't forget to download the video embed code in a blog post on your website to increase exposure and interaction — you may opt to embed the full status update or just the video player for a cleaner look.

Solicit Likes and Shares –invite your Page's Likers to do the same.

When you post, encourage users to 'Like' and Share your material so that it is spread on their walls and in their News Feeds, increasing your Page's exposure. Avoid appearing desperate by posting it too frequently (Facebook will limit the reach of these types of posts, especially if the material is terrible), and phrase it in a way that endears you to your fans. Make a direct request, and supporters will pay attention. Enhance the experience by establishing a community that stimulates discussion and interaction among your fans in the comments section.

Additionally, did you know that you can invite folks who have liked a post but not your Page to do so? When a post receives more than a handful of likes, it will display the message "[name], [name], [name], and [number] of others liked this." To view a list of everyone who liked that post and whether they liked your Page or not, click on the "others liked this" link (the chances are that many people will only see your post as a result of someone else engaging with it, and they being notified). If they haven't, you can click "Invite" next to their name to send them an invitation. If they've already loved your content, there's a better likelihood they'll be receptive to seeing it again.

Maintain a timely engagement

If someone leaves a comment on a status update or a public message on your wall, be careful to respond as quickly as possible. Any opportunity to continue the conversation, respond to a query, or express gratitude for a customer's support is effectively lost without a response - something that many businesses on Facebook fail to do to their harm. If your Page is overflowing and you lack time to respond to each fan comment, giving them a "like" (rather than dismissing them) demonstrates that you are paying attention to what they have to say.

Utilize @mentions to provide a personal touch and increase interaction.

When responding to comments made by specific fans on your Page, utilize the @username method to address each person personally. It will add a personal touch to your service and make the consumer feel unique, all the more so because they will receive notification that you responded. After typing @, immediately begin typing the person's name to whom you wish to reply. When their name appears, click or press it to pick it. If you want to be more informal and address a client solely by their first name, position your cursor at the end of their surname (after it appears in the comment box) and hit backspace several times until their surname vanishes. To that purpose, personalize any status updates or comments you make by 'signing' them with your first name; this is particularly handy if numerous administrators are addressing fans on the same page.

Include timeline milestones and leverage them as marketing opportunities.

By scrolling through and marking dates on your Timeline, Facebook enables you to add Milestones in the history of your business on your Page (e.g., when the business was established, your 1000th sale). These add context to your company's history and provide an intriguing glimpse into your growth over the months and years (mainly if you were in business way before Facebook rolled around). Additionally, you may use future milestones to interact with customers and present them with an incentive to stay connected, for example, "Here's to each of you for contributing to our 20,000-fan milestone! Return tomorrow at 6 p.m. for a special thank-you promotion!". Invite fans to share stories about how your product or service has improved their lives, and then include them - along with accompanying photographs - as milestones demonstrating how invested your consumers are in your business and encouraging others to do the same.

You should thank your newest fans and recognize a fan of the month.

Once a week, send a special 'Thank You're greeting to new fans, including their names if there aren't too many - you can discover them via the "See Likes" option in your Page's Admin Panel; this gives your communication a more personal touch and reflects your brand's image as one that cares about its audience. Launch a "Fan of the Month" initiative to increase your page's engagement. By promoting one of your most devoted fans in this manner, you indirectly inspire other fans to increase their engagement to compete for the coveted title the following month. As an added incentive, provide the winner with a little prize. Several free "Fan of the Month" apps are accessible via the Facebook search bar and commercial ones with additional features.

Chapter Five

The LinkedIn Market: Like a Clockwork, Create a Network

LinkedIn is the web's principal centre for individuals and businesses to connect and advertise their brand, expertise, and abilities to the rest of the world. It was founded in 2003 by Mark Zuckerberg and Reid Hoffman. If you are an individual on LinkedIn, the site can be used to establish a professional profile and control one of the top search results for your name, build a broad network of professional connections whose knowledge you can tap into, and discover new business opportunities, to name a few of the benefits. Creating a LinkedIn business platform allows businesses to communicate more information about themselves, their products and services, job opportunities, and expert insights with their target audiences. Any LinkedIn user can follow a firm that has created a Company Page to receive and interact with updates on their home page, which provides you with an opportunity to raise awareness of yourself and your brand among other LinkedIn users. In a study conducted by LinkedIn, it was discovered that you only need 100-200 followers of your Company Page to reach the tipping point where you can begin making an impact and driving engagement, so it's well worth your time to ensure that both it and your personal profile are performing at their best. Remember, many chapter tips are prefixed with either "Personal Profile" or "Company Pages," Some are prefixed with both. This can help you figure out how to put the advice you've received to good use. Whenever there is no prefix, the tip is a more general hint about one of the many things available on LinkedIn.

Now let us look into some techniques that will help optimize your page both as a personal page or as a Company page profile.

Company/Personal Profile Page Optimization.

LinkedIn Profile (Personal Profile and company profile):

Completely fill out the forms. Fill up all of the parts on your LinkedIn profiles, and make sure you have both a personal LinkedIn page for you as an individual and a LinkedIn Company Page that is mainly for your company - a LinkedIn Business Platform. As a result, you'll want to make a tremendous original outlook for any visitors who land on either of your landing pages.

Sections of your personal Profile that are extremely important:

One of the most significant sections of your personal LinkedIn profile is the Description section since it allows you to go into great detail about your current and previous jobs and responsibilities, as well as your accomplishments. This is a fantastic area to include some relevant keywords, which will increase your chances of ranking higher in LinkedIn's search results. Visitors will know what you've done at each of your positions with a short glance at your personal profile, and they will be able to discover more about you and decide whether you're someone they want to connect with to establish a new professional relationship with you. Short paragraphs or bullet-pointed lists can make a prospect's task even more accessible by making it easy for them to read. If you use bullets, begin your sentences with verbs to make them readable (past tense verbs for past positions, present-tense verbs for present functions). Rather than just pointing out what you did, Rather than just pointing out what you did, describe what you accomplished or how you contributed to the company's success. The more specific and precise you can be in this situation, the better. A vital component of your resume is the summary section, which provides you with your first opportunity to write an overview or statement about yourself and what you can offer your target audience, as well as a chance to demonstrate what makes you exclusive and alluring to potential contacts. Make sure that your Summary accurately reflects your personality. Your company website or LinkedIn Company Page indeed exists to inform people about your company, but your personal profile exists to allow LinkedIn users to discover more about you.

Understanding how to create a LinkedIn Business profile is paramount;

Now, to create a LinkedIn Business profile,

first, sign in as a personal user and then click on the "Companies" link in the navigation tab near the top of the site's home page.

From here, select the 'Add A Company' button, which is found at the top page on the right-hand side of the page. Before being allowed to begin using LinkedIn, there are a few modest milestones you must achieve and a few easy administrative formalities you must conquer, but you won't be waiting long until you're ready to go! Please keep in mind that to build a LinkedIn Business profile, you must first have a company email address, such as yourname@yourcompany.com. It is not authorized to use an email address that contains a domain name, such as Outlook or Gmail. You can begin adding info to your Business Page about your region, size, contact information, industry, and other relevant information by choosing Edit in the top-right hand corner of your company's Home tab after it has been created. Sections of the Company Page that are extremely important The

'Company Description' part is, without a doubt, the most crucial. Write a high-level description of your company that highlights your brand and informs readers about what distinguishes you from the competition. It is an excellent area to begin disseminating your message and contacting possible partners and collaborators. It's also a good idea to include a "Specialties" feature on your Business Profile overview. Complete the fields with terms that describe who you are and what you do to increase the likelihood of being discovered more frequently in a LinkedIn search result.

Showcase Pages for specialized items or services:

LinkedIn introduced Showcase Pages in November 2013. It was an interactive replacement for the former "Product and Services" tabs on the company product profile., withdrawn in April 2014. It was a big deal. Showcase Pages and Company Pages are not the same things, and they do not have all of the same features as one another.

Consider Showcase Pages to be the children of the parent website.

Companies can create Company Pages to broaden their LinkedIn presence by posting regular updates about a specific product/service/department/business initiative/etc. Rather than about their entire company as a whole. It also allows them to share unique and distinctive features of their brand with a more focused and targeted audience. Example: Microsoft has a primary Company Page and multiple Showcase Pages for particular products and services on its website. Training and certification in Microsoft Office and other Microsoft products. Showcase Pages can be followed and deliver updates to users the same way they can from any Company Page, so make sure you keep the high-quality content coming with photographs, links, videos, freebies, and other incentives. You should not hesitate to re-purpose an update if it appeals to both your more extensive fan base on your principal Company Page and a more niche audience on a Showcase Page. They have their own unique URL for easy sharing, and they also appear on the right-hand side of your Company Page, as shown in the example below. Following the identification of an area (or areas - you can build up to 10 Showcase Pages) of your organization for which a Showcase Page would be beneficial, the following is the procedure for creating a Showcase Page: Instructions on how to establish a Showcase Page are as follows:

1. Click the down arrow next to the coloured Modify button on the Business Page, then select "Create a Showcase Page."

2. Create a new Page and assign administrators to it by entering its name and clicking Create Page.

3. Select Create from the drop-down menu. The following are the optimal Showcase Page branding image sizes: The image for the hero (cover) should essentially be at a minimum of 974 × 330 pixels. The logo is 100 × 60 pixels in size. 50 x 50 pixels for a square logo.

Create a page for your personal profile and carrier for your company:

add a profile photo, a logo, and banner images to your website. Add a recent photo to your personal profile to humanize it - a surprising number of people fail to do so, much to their own cost. The dimensions of LinkedIn profile photos are 200 x 200 pixels. Keep it professional, though: don't put a picture of yourself in your bathing suit on the beach on your LinkedIn page; instead, publish a head and shoulders photo of yourself looking professional and presentable. With your personal information, keep your Profile photo up to date with your changing appearance, including hairstyles, glasses, clothing, and so on. This will ensure that you and your LinkedIn networks are easily identifiable during meetings, conferences, and other events you and your LinkedIn connections attend! In the summer of 2014, LinkedIn began rolling out cover photographs for personal profiles similar to Facebook. According to the guidelines, background photographs should be at least 1400 x 425 pixels in size. Make use of this space to highlight your brand personality, to help people understand who you are, what you do, and how you can assist them - ideas include a photo of yourself, your contact information (email, phone, Twitter handle, etc.), and a call to action (for example, a testimonial). The Home tab serves as the default landing page for your Business profile on LinkedIn, and it is here that your company logo and banner image will be displayed. However, the size is different from what you see on your Facebook cover image, which is reasonably close. The ideal size for a

LinkedIn cover image is 646 222 pixels; the profile photo, which is still square, but has been downsized to 50 x 50 pixels, is the same size as the cover image. Use this space to show and expand on your own branding message. Note: The Premium Content Bundle chapter of this book contains links to download Personal and Company page cover photo templates that are optimized for desktop and mobile displays (as well as a slew of other valuable resources).

Make your personal profile more client-oriented.

LinkedIn users' most common mistake is treating their personal profile as a virtual résumé, not the case. Most potential connections who come across you are not interested in learning about your educational background, your first job, or the accomplishments you have made so far. It is not sufficient to merely introduce yourself to guests. what you do, who you help, how they may help themselves or others in the Summary section at the upper section of your account page. It should also inform what others say about you (short, complimentary quote). Personal profile: think of a clever headline for it. Make your personal LinkedIn profile headline memorable and unique because it is the first piece of information a potential connection will notice about you. "Retail Manager" is a generic title that is not insufficient because millions of those are on LinkedIn. Consider what distinguishes you from others, what makes you unique, and what you want to be recognized for in the world.

Taking a more keen look at Profile Optimization on both personal and company levels, let us understand more steps that could be taken

1. Get a vanity URL for your personal profile. Create your LinkedIn URL of choice when editing your LinkedIn profile by going to the "public profile" area in the editing window. As with other social media platforms, this will

make sending potential clients to a memorable address much easier to accomplish.

2. Personal Profile: Make the most of your geographic area. It is possible that entering your location on LinkedIn is not as straightforward as it appears at first glance. If we consider the case of Merwyn, Illinois, which is a little town just outside of the much larger and better-known metropolis of Chicago - let us pretend for a moment that I am a resident of Merwyn for the purposes of this discussion. The fact that I have listed my location as Chicago will help me appear in more search results (if the search is filtered by location), and I will also be perceived as someone "local" to others in my target market if a prospect scouring LinkedIn was in charge of finding people from the Chicago land area. Consider how this technique might apply to

your particular situation and make the necessary changes to your profile.

3. Showcase your accomplishments in your personal profile. Users can add projects, languages, publications, awards, test scores, courses, patents, certifications, and volunteer work to their LinkedIn profiles. Users can also add photos to their profiles. As you can imagine, If you place yourself in the position of a potential partner, this will significantly enhance your profile in terms of both business and demonstrate your ability to be a well-rounded individual in your field of expertise. So, if you have any other information to share, please do so.

4. Personal Profile: Include rich visual information such as photographs and presentations in your profile. It is feasible to improve the appearance of your LinkedIn

profile by including visual content such as images, videos, infographics, and even Slidshare presentations. This will allow you to highlight your achievements, brands with which you have worked and benefited, your research, and your skills all at the same time. Popular blog entries, screenshots of customer testimonials (such as a tweet or product review), or a video of a fantastic speech you gave at a conference are all examples of unique content to include. Simply click to edit your profile, then click the "+" symbol next to any employment opportunity you're interested in, and then pick whether to upload a file or share a link with other people. It's a no-brainer whenever it concerns Slideshare; you may share an uploaded presentation directly to your LinkedIn profile's Summary section by selecting "Add to profile" from the dropdown menu that displays when you hover over a presentation in the "My Uploads" part of Slideshare. When you upload new slideshows, the same choice will be available to you.

5. Personal Profile and Company Pages: Use points to make your pages easier to read. If you've completed your LinkedIn profile as its whole, you've likely included a significant amount of information, some of which (achievements, duties, and so on) would be much easier for prospects to read if they were organized in a bulleted list. Although you can use bullet points in your LinkedIn profile sections, this isn't something that the company promotes publicly. Here's how it's done:

- Log into LinkedIn, and from the log option at the top of the screen, pick "Page Edit."
- Navigate to the Profile part where you wish to include bullet points and select the pencil icon.

- "•" should be typed at the beginning of the line to put a bullet point (without the speech marks). You can go through this process as many times as you desire, then click Save.

- You're finished, and your text should be bulleted for easy reading. You might not be allowed to detect the "•" code if you return to edit a section where you have added bullets since it has been replaced with a single space at the beginning of a new line. To get rid of the bullet, delete this space and then hit the Save button.

6. Create your personal profile and company pages with keywords relevant to your company or industry. When you optimize your LinkedIn pages with keywords relevant to you, your expertise, and your business, your pages have a better chance of ranking higher in Google and LinkedIn search results than

when they are not optimized. Keep it subtle by not writing in an unnatural style that makes it evident to readers that you are attempting to cram in as many keywords as possible - but be mindful that you'll want to include them regardless of how subtle your writing style is. It's significant to mention in your Profile whenever you gain new skills or knowledge. Fill in as many skills as you can because LinkedIn allows you to add up to 50 skills in total. As a result, you should employ a variety of keywords ranging from broad ones to those that are more specialized, as you never know what search terms someone else may be used to potentially find you. It is also important where you place these keywords - according to a study conducted by blogging4jobs.com, the terms associated with your name, headline, company name, job title, and talents rank the most. Another crucial area of your personal LinkedIn profile where you should include keywords is the job experience section, including your current and previous roles. Explain your objectives and purpose in considerable detail, going into the same level of detail you would put on your resume. Include any accomplishments and goals that you have met or exceeded. Don't be scared to exaggerate a little!

7. Personal Profile: Rearrange the value of employment roles in your life. By default, LinkedIn will arrange your job positions in chronological order; however, by tapping on the up and down arrow icons beside any position and then picking and releasing it into whatever order you prefer, you can override the system and arrange them according to importance to you (and potential connections).

8. Marketing on LinkedIn and content strategy

   Personal Profile: Employee profiles can promote your company's image. Getting all of your employees on board with your LinkedIn strategy is critical to its success because it allows you to build a more extensive network that increases your company's visibility and influence on the social media platform. Instruct your staff to build their LinkedIn profiles and mention your company as their employer on their profiles. As a last resort, provide them with training on creating a great LinkedIn profile. Instead of being concerned that their company's employee profiles will make them a target for headhunters from competing companies, consider them as a reflection of your company's exceptional performance. It is likely that many of your employees already have LinkedIn profiles, and unfortunately, there isn't much you can do to prevent them from leaving if they so choose -

the best thing to do is to focus on the positives.

9. Personal Profile: I am a follower of various businesses. Company followers make it easy for you to keep an eye on important events occurring at firms you are interested in, which helps keep tabs on the competition and find inspiration for yourself. From a company's Company Page, you may choose whether or not to follow them. To keep up with a company:

   a. From the log option at the top of your site, select Companies.
   b. Look for a company to work for.
   c. On the company's Home page, click the Follow button in the upper right corner.

   Follow these steps to cease following a company:

- Slide down to the Following section of your Profile after selecting Profile from the log menu at the top of your site.
- To reveal more company details in the Companies section, move your pointer over the preceding grey link below the company's name.
- From the log option, click "Unfollow".

10. Personal Profile: Use Advanced Search and Get Introduced to locate prospects and gain trust, leading to sales or collaboration opportunities. The search and Advanced Search options on LinkedIn are excellent tools for identifying and connecting with possible new prospects. You can narrow down your results by relationships, groups, industry, and region, and you can even store your search for future reference. Even if you cannot connect with someone directly on LinkedIn, you may be able to gather enough

information to contact them outside of the platform, such as through their website or another social profile. Take note that if you click on the "Connect" button next to someone's name in a LinkedIn search, your invitation will be issued automatically, and you will not be given the ability to personalize your message, which is an enormous mistake. Ensure that you click on the person's profile and click the "Connect" button that appears. From here, a box will emerge for you to fill out to create a unique invitation - more information on the best method will be provided shortly. Keep in mind to check the "Persons Who Viewed This Page" box in the righthand sidebar for other people who might make outstanding prospects! Alternative options include utilizing the Get Introduced feature. Contacting members of LinkedIn who are in our 2nd or 3rd-degree network is made possible as a result of this feature. Here's how it's done:

a. Select " Get acquainted through a connection " from the Send, In Mail drop-down menu on the person you wish to connect with, select "Get acquainted through a connection" from the log menu. Should only one of you introduce, the Request an Introduction page will appear. To get introduced, move your mouse pointer over the arrow next to the Send-In Mail button and select Get introduced. If several individuals are capable of making the introduction, you have the option of selecting the person who will make the introduction.

b. Create and send a message to your recipient. When people want to connect with you, be thoughtful and kind in your response. Do the same when you want to connect with others - but avoid being pushy! If you want to customize your invitation, greet them by name and include a brief message that demonstrates that you read and loved a blog post they authored or a lecture they gave in which you were in attendance.

Completing your invitation by providing a compelling cause for you and your guest to engage with one another is recommended. It is possible to make an excellent first impression by including these little extras, which will boost your chances of starting a relationship with someone you are interested in. Once you have established a successful connection with a prospect, write a brief thank-you note and then engage in further conversation to help the relationship grow. Follow-up strategies will change depending on the reasons you linked in the first place and your ultimate goals. Here are some examples: Ideally, you don't want to start pitching your service or product straight away; instead, spend some time getting to know your prospect, possibly by identifying a similarity between you based on the information on their Profile. Simply putting up a reminder utilizing the LinkedIn Contacts tool to "touch base" for several weeks or delivering a free quote, PDF, or another beneficial resource from the goodness of your heart could be enough to make a positive impression. You might consider expanding the conversation to other social media platforms and offline as a method to move things forward toward your end objective, such as offering a product or service or forging a meaningful collaboration, after the relationship has grown sufficiently strong.

11. Personal Profile: Accept invitations that are of high quality and relevance. Along with looking for opportunities to interact with people, you should accept invitations from those who wish to connect with you. The more connections you have, the better. The more

comprehensive your expanded network becomes, which in turn opens the door to new opportunities down the road. Unfortunately, spammers can be found on LinkedIn, as they can be found on many social media platforms, so be cautious to only accept invitations from credible and appropriate profiles.

12. Utilize tags and notes to neatly manage your connections on your personal profile page. The Contacts function on LinkedIn (which can be reached via the Networks option) displays a list of all of your relationships on the social networking site. Tagging individuals with specific characteristics with unique labels is one of its uses. By doing so, You'll have the opportunity to categorize and organize different types of individuals (such as hot prospects, existing clients, thought leaders, and so on) to sort, find, and contact them as

quickly and efficiently as possible whenever the need arises. Simply click on the tag icon to the right of a contact's name, select from the suggested tags list, or create your own. After that, you may use the Tags option to filter connections based on their tags. When you click on a contact's complete Profile, you will see a "Relationship" option, denoted by a star. This is an additional step in improving organization and efficiency. There are various options available when you click this, including an area to make comments about that person, a place to add how you met, and a function to create reminders about them, such as when you need to follow up with them. Each piece of information in this part is only accessible by you. Please keep in mind that your Contacts page will also notify you of critical developments in the professional lives of your connections, such as when they begin a new position. Remember to send a brief letter to express your appreciation for a contact's accomplishment, stay in touch, and continue strengthening your relationship.

Chapter Six
Pinterest as a Media Platform

Pinterest permits anyone to fashion and establish virtual pinboards on virtually any theme, and then stake these pins (which are most frequently images but can also be in video form) with other Pinterest operators as well as with individuals all over the globe via websites, blogs, and other social networks. Alternatively, pins can be posted directly from your computer or mobile device, or they can be shared through a website. Pinterest's popularity has skyrocketed since the site's introduction in March of 2010. As a result, when you consider that Pinterest is the second most important driver of web traffic among social media sites (behind only Facebook), it should come as no surprise that tens of thousands of businesses, including the world's largest, are already utilizing the site to showcase their brand to an audience of over 70 million users, with more than 75 per cent of those users accessing the site via mobile devices. Pinterest users come to the site to search for, browse, and collect the things that fascinate and inspire them - and it is here that the enormous potential for companies on the site comes into play, as many of them are shoppers. Individual or business, the most successful Pinterest pins all have a few things in common: they combine eye-catching photos with information that solves a problem, inspires a user, offers something valuable, or appeals to a user's interest in a certain hobby or activity. Contemplate how these pinnable characteristics can be applied to your brand as a way for people to discover content about the things they love that you have previously pinned - to encourage engagement and conversation about your company culture, products, and services, and to drive click-through rates to your content that isn't hosted on the Pinterest platform. If a vendor of bespoke dog collars publishes pins on how to teach dogs tricks or how to make homemade dog treats, this is an example of affiliate marketing. While some Pinterest users come to the site with the express intent of finding a product to purchase, others do not or are at a different stage of the purchasing process.

***

As a result, the combination of content you supply should be appealing to and beneficial to both types. To summarize: If the content you post inspires someone to purchase from you, that's fantastic (Pinterest users frequently create "wish list boards" as a stepping stone to purchasing products, so you'll want to encourage them to add your products to these while browsing), but if it makes them laugh, smile, daydream, or think positively about you, that's also fantastic. Pins that are not just promotional in nature but also lifestyle-based and influential due to their good association with your company can be just as useful in the long term as promotional pins. Whether your material provides a useful suggestion or inspires a user to take action, it will only increase the likelihood that they will repin it to one of their boards for safekeeping and display it to their followers via their Home screens, as described above. If you have a passion for inspiring people with words and photos, you should use Pinterest, no matter what type of business you have. Demonstrate their objectives and dreams to them. This means that you should create boards that highlight your products and services and boards that demonstrate fascinating and pinnable ideas, topics, and concepts related to your products and services. Although your company might not be particularly very visually oriented and you, on the other hand, might not believe Pinterest would be a good fit for your needs, it's important to realize that the site is as much (if not more) about collecting and sharing photos created by others as it is about pinning your own. For example, a coffee shop might include a board with information on their drinks and food and the newest trends in coffee culture - gadgets, music, interior design, and so on - on which customers can comment. People re-pin and follow accounts on Pinterest because they are relevant to their interests and needs, not because they are enthusiastic about your latest marketing effort! Be a resource for pinners and approach your pins with a service mindset rather than a profit-driven one. Optimization of your Pinterest profile Although Pinterest's present structure does not provide a great deal of flexibility for altering the appearance of your profile, there are still a few important things you should consider doing to maximize the impact of your account... Become a registered business (or adapt your private Pinterest profile account) Since its launch in November

2012, Pinterest has increased its support for brands, including the ability for them to register specifically as businesses (rather than just as individuals), putting into consideration also, the ability for those brands that already had a Pinterest presence to convert their personal accounts to business accounts. To do either, go to http://business.pinterest.com and select the one that pertains to you from the drop-down menu.

***

Once you've registered as a business on Pinterest, you'll have access to a variety of business-specific resources, such as Pinterest analytics tools, successful case studies, and links to Pinterest buttons and widgets that you can use to advertise your activity on the site on your website or blog. Make a memorable username for yourself. When creating a Pinterest account, the first thing you'll want to make sure you get right is your username, which will serve as the basis for your Pinterest profile's URL. You will want to market this URL online and in-person, making it as short, straightforward, and memorable as possible. Although your brand image is the most logical alternative, examine whether or not you have a keyword or slogan associated with it that would work better (especially if your brand's name is larger than the 15-character restriction). Furthermore, your 'First Name' and 'Last Name' must reflect your brand because they will be shown prevalently somewhere at the top of your Pinterest account. For example, I may go by the identities 'The Social media market strategist' and 'Marketing Tips, as my first and last names. Although, if your organization's name is short, it may not be required to include the last name. Make use of the information in the 'About' section. If you create a detailed description in the About area of Pinterest, it will be located precisely at the top-right of your profile page and serves to describe your brand and what you do. Aside from showing up more frequently in your search result, you must include two or three of your company's most important keywords in the description under your Pinterest URL. Don't go overboard with the character count - 160 characters should be sufficient. Add your website and check it for trustworthiness before submitting it. This one is very self-explanatory. When someone visits your profile, a small 'globe' icon will be displayed at the very top of the page, which, when clicked, will take them to your website. It isn't prominently displayed on the Pinterest profile page, but every little bit helps, so don't forget to fill it out. You can authenticate your website on Pinterest to show others that you are a trustworthy source of information. Once you've validated your account in your profile, you'll see a checkmark next to the URL. As well as access to Pinterest site analytics. To have your website verified on Pinterest, simply click the "Verify Website" button that appears next to the field where you typed your website's URL. Follow the on-screen directions to finish the verification procedure on the following page. Verification can be accomplished by using an HTML file or a meta tag. Create an eye-catching profile picture. Your company's insignia and, if you're the company's figurehead, a head and shoulders shot of yourself are the two most prevalent types of Pinterest profile photographs for brands - of course, smiling and looking pleased. Pinterest profile photographs are displayed within a rounded square on your profile page, as well as within circles adjacent to pinned content and comments, and within circles next to pinned comments. Ensure that your brand is visible in the centre of the 200 by 200-pixel image and keep your company logo or face within the middle "safe region," away from the corners, to guarantee that it looks excellent anywhere it appears on the site. Download a prototype to help you do so (as well as a slew of other useful resources) from the Premium Content Bundle chapter of this book. Strategy for using Pinterest as a marketing and content distribution channel Following the completion of your Pinterest profile page, let's look at the marketing and content tactics that will assist you in taking advantage of every possibility that the platform has to offer. Optimum The dimensions and design of Pinterest pin images Pinterest does not impose any restrictions on the vertical dimension of photographs pinned to its boards, but the horizontal width of images is limited to 735 pixels at the most. Any image width is acceptable; however, It would be adjusted to a maximum resolution of 735 pixels and shown as such. Also, keep to heart the following: Pinterest only allows users to pin from web pages that have at least one image, and these photos must be a minimum dimension of 110 x 110 pixels to be permitted to pin. To encourage others to pin from your website or blog, include at minimum one pinnable image on every page or article. The use of taller photos on Pinterest, according to research, results in more re-pins because they work better with the way the site stacks different pieces of material on top of each other in its infinitely-scrolling, narrowly barred grid. As a result, if you want your photographs on your Pinterest account and blog to be shared more frequently on Pinterest, make them as tall as possible. Naturally, this isn't always practical, but there are several simple methods to include this strategy into your Pinterest activity using picture kinds like infographics and step-by-step "how-to" posts (both of which are detailed below). When it comes to colour and design, a year-long study by Curalate, a Philadelphia-based startup, found that images (particularly of products) taken against a plain and minimalist background performed better on Pinterest (in contrast to most other social networks) than those with too much in the frame (in contrast to most other social networks). Additionally, photos that are too light or too dark were shown to perform poorly - images in the centre of the spectrum performed best. Pins that had numerous dominating colours (rather than just one) were observed to garner greater attention, while bright and warm colours such as orange and red were observed to be re-pinned more frequently than "colder" colours such as blue were observed to receive less attention. And last but not least, it discovered that photographs without human faces performed best on Pinterest - arguing that this is because the site is a social media platform of "things," where faces are merely a distraction, as opposed to sites such as Facebook, which is a type of social media interconnection of people. I propose that you take these trends with a grain of salt and keep a careful eye on which material works best for you and your target audience as you create your Pinterest strategy. When and what to pin - Maintain a consistent and innovative approach. Pin on a steady and regular basis - a few times a day is a good goal - but keep the stream moving steadily, rather than letting it go for weeks with no activity followed by a flurry of activity. This method will increase your exposure and prevent your followers from being inundated with messages. If you want to increase the exposure of your Pinterest content, don't be afraid to pin it more than once. Don't pin it to the same board repeatedly (choose one with a similar fit or a group board), and don't pin it immediately after the initial share - always give the original pin time to shine before pinning again. What you publish will be determined by your business or company, but given that studies show that approximately 80% of Pinterest's content comprises re-pinned pins, make an effort to generate original and exciting pins to guarantee that you are included in the magical other 20% of the content. Using the following method when posting a pin that involves a product may be beneficial: one photo of the product on its own (for example, with a simple white background) and another photo of the product in the environment where it will be utilized (e.g., luxury towels in a bathroom). The former technique allows followers to picture how the product can fit into their lives, while the latter allows them to pin basic photos for inspiration. Remember to link both pins to the same sales page on your website, as well as the other way around. When you share information from others, you can establish yourself as an authority in your field by sharing motivational content. Engaging, accurate, up-to-date, helpful, and insightful content. In addition to being an advertisement for your brand, other Pinterest users' boards tell a great deal about their likes, interests, hopes, and aspirations. Make the most of this knowledge to transform your profile into a destination that benefits your audience. Select "Popular" from the drop-down menu on the Pinterest home page to learn more about what's popular with Pinterest users right now, and then determine whether it is appropriate for you to incorporate these trends into your content strategy: Share pins from other boards that your followers will love to make your profile a more valuable asset. Note: Pinterest uses a "smart feed" algorithm to determine the distinction of a pin is built on the beauty of the image it contains and the management structure of the website from which it was pinned - The quality of a pin is determined by the number of people that pin it on the site. Pins that combine these two characteristics are preferred in the site's feed because they are more visually appealing. It's hard to know whether or not your pins are being singled out for special treatment by the smart feed algorithm, but being aware of this back-end procedure should motivate you to regularly share only the greatest content. Keep the names of your boards short and simple. Even while you should use keyword-rich titles for your boards, you should make the names basic and descriptive so they can be found readily in Pinterest's search - yet short enough so that the names do not trail off when viewed on your profile. When viewed on your profile page, each of your board names can have up to 30 or so characters (including spaces) before being cut off - the remaining characters can be seen when the board is clicked on. In contrast, the cut-off point for Pinterest searches is significantly shorter, at roughly 20 characters. If the name of your message board is more than 20 characters, attempt to include the most relevant keywords at the beginning of the name to increase the likelihood that other users will notice it. It's critical to select your Pinterest account theme precisely because it will become part of its URL, i.e., www.pinterest.com/your-board-name (important for SEO). Note: Because several individuals use Pinterest as a search engine (in some cases, preferring it over Google for specific searches), approaching the setup of your content on the site with an SEO mindset is important - in board names, pin names and descriptions, and even the file name of your images - is important (more on these shortly). Keep the term "niche" in mind when establishing boards. While browsing Pinterest, you may have noticed that some of the most well-known brands have built a large number of pinboards, each of which contains content that is highly relevant to the brand's identity. However, while overloading your profile with pins may seem counter-intuitive to the "less is more" school of thought, it may actually prove beneficial in the long run. Why? Because several individuals use Pinterest search to find content (or come across it via a web search), having highly targeted boards increases the likelihood that your pins will be discovered and viewed. Consider the following example: a board titled "Wedding Inspiration" is highly general - there are thousands of other boards with the same name, and the chances of yours getting discovered if you are just starting out as a wedding accessories dealer are poor. Although less likely to be looked for, a board called "Pink Wedding Dresses 2014" has significantly less competition, giving it a greater chance of being discovered in search results than a board called "White Wedding Dresses 2014." So, while creating your Pinterest boards, think about what makes them distinct, particular, and niche, and target the material and phrases you believe your target audience will be looking for. Choose a visually appealing board cover. As a board cover, one pin from each of your Pinterest boards will be selected from your collection of pins. Your profile picture and search results should have eye-catching, beautiful, and accurately represent the board as a whole. In a nutshell, your board cover should entice people enough to make them want to click on it and read the entire material. To choose a pin as the cover for a board on your profile, hover over the board in question and click the 'Change Cover' button on your keyboard. Use the arrows to navigate to the pin you want to use as the cover for your board. When choosing your board cover image, you have the option of repositioning the image so that the best section of the image is seen on the cover. To make the modification effective, click Save Changes. Reorganize your Pinterest boards according to their value. Pinterest gives you the ability to reorganize the boards on your profile page. It's as simple as clicking, holding, and dragging boards into their optimal placements from your profile page. The aim here is to move your most significant boards to the first few rows - particularly those that are 'above the fold,' that is, visible onscreen before a user has to scroll down to access more boards. Consider which of your boards you want to highlight the most prominently - whether it's based on seasonal promotions, holidays, current trends, or anything else - and place them in the most important real estate regions of your Pinterest profile, such as the header and footer. Create secret boards to collect pins and strategize marketing campaigns. Create an unlimited number of secret boards that can be made public at any moment in the future with

Pinterest's 'Secret Boards' function. One simple and effective application of Secret Boards is seasonal marketing, such as Valentine's Day, Thanksgiving, Christmas, and other holidays. As you slowly accumulate content for your campaign's themed Secret Board throughout the year, you'll be well prepared to make it public when the time comes. You'll have a ton of material to choose from, and then you can continue to add to it during the campaign's promotional period. To create a Secret Board, choose the option located at the extreme lower part of your homepage; or, when creating a board from the 'Add' menu, be sure to toggle the Secret Board slider to the 'On' position as described above. Effective pin descriptions will increase re-pins and web traffic. Pinterest is one of the most important website traffic sources globally; creating excellent pin descriptions is critical to providing your content with the best possible chance of getting discovered when a user searches the site.

Since the launch of Pinterest's Guided Search in April 2014, optimizing your pin descriptions has become even more important (a feature that provides fast keyword ideas and inspiration to assist users in discovering exactly what they are looking for). The primary recommendation is to come up with the best pin captions in the manner of a useful and searchable piece of information, including specific and distinct keywords that reflect the pin's content and your business, for example, "red, V-neck striped red sweater from Karen's Apparel, Denver" is much more effective than simply "wool sweater." As a rule, if the pin requires it, descriptions that explain how the subject of the pin adds value function better than direct explanations, so think about what a potential buyer might want to know and write with that in mind. Instead of saying something like "We're now selling these diamond earrings, let us know what you think of them," a more effective description might read something like, "The way that the light bounces off these beautiful diamond earrings is mesmerizing, and they'd look great with just about any outfit for a night out on the town. "

In your pin description, provide a call to action. According to some studies, it can help increase the number of clicks on your pin, so you may want to include one in your description.

Conclusion

In modern days, the things you can accomplish with social media are almost endless, and that limitation can only exist in your imagination. To sum up, you will agree with me that we are better off now than we were ten years ago in terms of marketing and placing items into a wider viewing range. The Internet has already changed people's lives, and social media has contributed to that optimism by making selling and buying faster and more efficient, making product providers' and sellers' jobs easier. This will work for those prepared to put in the effort, and it will be a massive money-making operation.